Connected Librarians

Tap Social Media to Enhance Professional Development and Student Learning

Nikki D Robertson

International Society for Technology in Education

PORTLAND, OREGON • ARLINGTON, VIRGINIA

Connected Librarians
Tap Social Media to Enhance Professional Development
and Student Learning
Nikki D Robertson

© 2017 International Society for Technology in Education
World rights reserved. No part of this book may be reproduced or transmitted in any form or by any means—electronic, mechanical, photocopying, recording, or by any information storage or retrieval system—without prior written permission from the publisher. Contact Permissions Editor: iste.org/about/permissions-and-reprints; permissions@iste.org; fax: 1.541.302.3780.

Editor: *Emily Reed*
Copy Editor: *Karstin Painter*
Proofreader: *Corinne Gould*
Book Design and Production: *Kim McGovern*
Cover Design: *Edwin Ouellette*

Library of Congress Cataloging-in-Publication Data available.

First Edition
ISBN: 978-1-56484-392-0
Ebook version available.

Printed in the United States of America

ISTE® is a registered trademark of the International Society for Technology in Education.

About ISTE

The International Society for Technology in Education (ISTE) is the premier nonprofit organization serving educators and education leaders committed to empowering connected learners in a connected world. ISTE serves more than 100,000 education stakeholders throughout the world.

ISTE's innovative offerings include the ISTE Conference & Expo, one of the biggest, most comprehensive events in the world—as well as the widely adopted ISTE Standards for learning, teaching and leading in the digital age and a robust suite of professional learning resources, including webinars, online courses, consulting services for schools and districts, books, and peer-reviewed journals and publications. Visit iste.org to learn more.

Join our community of passionate educators

ISTE members get free year-round professional development opportunities and discounts on ISTE resources and conference registration. Membership also connects you to a network of educators who can instantly help with advice and best practices.

Join or renew your ISTE membership today! Visit iste.org/membership or call 800.336.5191.

About the Author

Nikki D. Robertson is a veteran educator, school librarian, instructional technology facilitator, and ISTE Librarians Network President Elect. Nikki is passionate about 1:1 digital initiatives, collaboration with other education professionals, and assisting students in becoming well informed, critically thinking digital citizens.

Nikki D. Robertson
@NikkiDRobertson

Nikki is the co-founder of the first EdCamp Atlanta (edcampatlanta.org), a free "un-conference" committed to reaching educators in public, private, charter, and higher ed environments to share innovative instructional strategies and pioneering technologies that transform education for all students.

Nikki has also collaborated in the creation of and moderation of free national and global professional development designed specifically for the unique needs of school librarians, including #TLChat LIVE! Twitter chat sessions, and TL News Night, a LIVE Internet show presented in news show format featuring a wrap-up of "This Month in School Libraries" and deeper discussion of topical school library issues with special guest experts.

Nikki is the recipient of several honors, including an ASLA Ann Marie Pipkin Technology Award and the AASL Bound to Stay Bound Grant.

Nikki is a frequent presenter at library and educational technology conferences, including ISTE, METC (Midwest Education Technology Conference), NCCE (Northwest Council for Computer Education), TLA (Texas Library Association Conference) Model Schools Conference, SimpleK12, FETC

(Florida Educational Technology Conference), EdSpeakers Group, and many more.

Other Titles in the Digital Age Librarian's Series

Reimagining Library Spaces: Transform Your Space on Any Budget, by Diana Rendina

Inspiring Curiosity: The Librarian's Guide to Inquiry-Based Learning, by Colette Cassinelli

To see all books available from ISTE, please visit iste.org/resources.

Acknowledgments

Thanks to my professional learning community and the individuals who have inspired this book by embracing the power of social media. Thanks especially to the following cast of characters who directly influenced this book. They are valuable sources of information and worthy additions to your own learning communities.

Jennifer Hogan
@Jennifer_Hogan

Daniel Whitt
@WhittMister

Holly Sutherland
@DrHSutherland

Molly Wetta
@molly_wetta

Matt Miller
@jmattmiller

Jennifer Woodruff Brower
@CybrarianJenn

Rachel Murat
@MrsMurat

Eric Neuman
@EricNeuman

Gwyneth Jones
@GwynethJones

Anastasia Hanneken
@21stcentlib

Jane Lofton
@jane_librarian

Laura Gardner
@LibrarianMsG

Jerry Blumgarten
@Cybraryman

AJ Bianco
@AJBianco

Wendy Cope
@wendypcope

Julie Boatner
@jboatner

Contents

Preface

Tiffany Whitehead (@librarian_tiff), also known to many as the Mighty Little Librarian (mightylittlelibrarian.com), was the catalyst behind the creation of this book. I am deeply grateful that she entrusted me to see this work she started through to the end, and can only hope that I do it justice.

After twenty-five years as an educator, I cannot say that there are many professional books that have thrilled me as the likes of a J. K. Rowling or Mary Roach book. I have found most to be dry and clinical. Quite frankly, concepts presented in professional books seemed unrealistic when I tried to apply them in a school setting.

It is my intention to provide within each chapter a brief overview of the designated topic, followed by real-life examples of how each type of social media can be incorporated into your library or school in simple and stress-free ways.

However, because technologies can change on a dime—existing one moment and gone the next—I advise you to let the ideas shared in this book spark your inspiration for how to use social media in your own school, as well as how to apply these or similar ideas to new and emerging technologies.

While reading this book, please keep in mind the ISTE Standards for Educators and Students. These standards provide a framework for rethinking learning and teaching in the digital age. With standards like "Empowered Learner," "Innovative Designer," and "Creative Communicator," the standards directly address strategies for effectively incorporating social media tools. The ISTE Student and Educator Standards are found in Appendix A.

The Power of Social Media

Remember playing word association games? One person says a word or phrase, and the other person states the first word that comes to their mind. Let's play that game now, but let's stick to the subject of education. If I say, "social media," what is the first word that pops into your mind? Did you think of any words like those below?

Distraction	Blocked
Silliness	Sexting
Juvenile	Bullying
Inappropriate	Digital citizenship

Or, does your mind take you to words like these?

Connecting	Access
Learning	Growth
Sharing	Knowledge
Real-world connections	

What we think about social media in schools is influenced by our own experiences with the education system; our values—and even our biases—are reflected in our assessments of school programs. If the first set of words resonated the loudest with you, I hope the contents of this book will do more than merely change these word associations for you; I hope they will assist you in convincing others in your district that social media is a valuable, powerful educational tool for students and staff.

I Have a *Real* Job to Do

School librarians' roles have changed drastically, especially within the last ten years, as the influx of technology has worked its way into our school systems. Once viewed as the guardians, organizers, lenders, and recommenders of books and other resources—magically appearing from the stacks or the elusive "back office"—school librarians today are thought and technology leaders. It is important that, as leaders, we have a solid understanding of social media, maintain our own personal and professional online presences, and help educators, administrators, students, and parents use social media to both enhance professional development and empower student learning.

Unfortunately, there are still many among us who have failed to see the ways that social media can pique the personal genius in both our teachers and our students, inspiring new projects and ways of engaging with content and one another. At a recent school library conference, I was taking Snapchat selfies with attendees to show off the app's new geolocation filters. You can use these filters to help promote and engage students in special events at your school or library. Upon seeing this, one attendee commented, "I don't have time for social media. I have a real job to do."

Instead of feeling angry or insulted, I actually understood where that comment was coming from. I had been in the same frame of mind not so many years ago. Librarians are stretched thin and social media can seem like yet another chore. In reality, social media is the perfect companion tool for a great many things we already do in our school libraries.

Not My Thing, Not My Job.

In this era of shrinking budgets, school libraries are increasingly on the chopping block with reduced hours, clerks replacing certified librarians, and even permanent closure. The crowd-sourced Google map, A Nation without School Libraries (goo.gl/jv4PbF), began to document cuts to school libraries in one form or another beginning in 2010; the map has unfortunately continued to grow each year since.

One of the most effective ways school librarians can stem the tide of cuts and ensure our libraries stay intact is by telling the stories of how the library positively impacts student learning and enhances teacher instruction. Social media provides the perfect platform for sharing these stories beyond passing conversations in the hallway or teachers' lounge, where they can reach a larger audience that includes parents, community members, and legislators who ultimately control the flow of funding to schools and school libraries. Telling the stories of our school libraries isn't bragging—it's a celebration of the learning that is taking place in our schools. The stories are proof that an active, appropriately funded library with a certified school librarian is vital to our school communities.

Rising from the Ashes

Much like the conference attendee I referenced earlier, the power of social media wasn't initially obvious to me. In the mid-2000s, I attended a state library conference session about getting connected with Twitter. I sat, listened, opened up a Twitter account, and then did nothing with it for over a year. I wondered what all the fuss was about. I had a Twitter account, yet nothing had changed. I concluded that Twitter just must not be my "thing."

Then, a strange combination of circumstance, curiosity, and timing changed my mind about social media, and especially Twitter. Through the 2008–10 school years, I began noticing odd-looking squares on the periodicals routinely ordered for the school library. I noticed them on pages featuring advertisements, but also on signs in stores, at bus stops, and anywhere advertisements were placed. My curiosity got the better of me one day and I did a little research to find out what the squares were, and why they were now appearing in the majority of our school library periodicals. It didn't take long to discover that the odd squares were called QR codes, and that businesses were using them to attract potential purchasers by offering an interactive experience.

This made sense to me. Advertising companies are always competing for attention from a fast-moving, short-attention-spanned demographic; finding ways to capture and hold their customers' attention means the difference between those customers not only remembering the product, but associating it with positive feelings.

What didn't occur to me, and what now feels like one of my bigger "duh" moments, was that I had been working with a fast-moving, short-attention-spanned demographic since 1992, when I first became an educator! Other educators had put these thoughts together and, by the time I had first started researching QR codes, had already begun using them to captivate young minds, enhance instruction, and engage student learning. My feelings of joy were soon overtaken by anger and resentment toward the school district I worked for.

I am ashamed to admit that, from the early 90s until the early 2000s, I had been "that" educator—the one who passively waited for the school or district to provide professional learning. Even worse, I was the one who attended conferences to ensure I had enough professional development hours to keep my teaching certification up to date, yet I often dismissed the presenters, almost priding myself on my uncanny ability to pick apart their presentations. When I discovered other educators across the country knew about QR codes and had been using them to successfully engage students in learning, I was resentful because no one at my school, district, or any conferences I had attended had ever even mentioned QR codes, much less how they could be used in an educational setting.

The audacity that no one had introduced me to QR codes propelled me to find out why certain districts had provided timely and useful professional development for their educators, while others had not. What I discovered resulted in a landslide of positive change and opened my eyes to the power of social media.

The first thing I discovered in my search was that I had been asking the wrong question. It wasn't the school districts that had provided information about QR codes. These educators had learned about QR codes on their own or through other educators who were interested in how QR codes could be used to entice students to pay attention and learn. Again, the ability to put two and two together didn't immediately click, and I discovered sometime later that the key to all of this was community; these educators were willing to connect, share, learn, and grow—together.

I began my search for more relevant professional learning online. Almost immediately, I came across websites offering astronomically expensive (and horribly dry) professional development opportunities for educators, but specialized online courses for school librarians were virtually impossible to find. I was beginning to feel defeated in my quest when I happened across a website called The 30 Goals Challenge for Educators (livebinders.com/play/play?id=442965&present=true), created by Shelly Terrell. The site was simple, easy to understand, welcoming, and it was *free*! At first, I was worried that I had missed the start date for joining in the thirty challenges but was quickly reassured that the only requirement was to simply *try*. I wasn't required to do all the goals or start in any particular order. It was my choice to review the thirty goals presented and start in a place where I felt comfortable enough to step out of my comfort zone.

One of the first goals I chose was Goal 10: Make A Connection. This goal attracted my attention because it used Twitter, and I had an account that had been sitting there, mute and idle. I was also attracted to this goal because it reminded me of the teachers who had been using QR codes in their schools, classrooms, and libraries. Goal 10 introduced ways I could use various social media venues to make connections and showed me how, by doing this, I could build a Professional Learning Network (PLN). I soon learned about a new Twitter chat started by Shelly Terrell (@ShellTerrell), Jerry Blumengarten (@cybraryman1), and Tom Whitby (@tomwhitby) that used the hashtag #EdChat. I used this as my catalyst to work through Goal 10.

Tuesdays soon became my favorite day of the week as I anticipated participating in the #EdChat conversations. Never, in all my years as an educator, had I been part of such a stimulating, thought provoking dialogue with other education professionals. Going to sleep on a Tuesday night was virtually impossible as my head buzzed with new ideas that I could take back and implement in my school library.

Every connected educator with whom I had conversed had classrooms and schools that seemed to be amazing hubs of learning, engagement, innovation, and fun. After a few months of engaging in weekly #EdChat conversations, I thought my life as a newly connected educator was going to be sunshine, rainbows, and lollipops. The experience for me, however, was different.

Burned Out and Drifting

Let's stop for a minute and go back in time to before my QR code journey led to Shelly Terrell's 30 Goals Challenge and the #EdChat Twitter chat. At this point in my career, I had been sculpted from an eager, energetic, new teacher to an educator who was basically doing the bare minimum to collect a paycheck. Year after year of beating my head against institutional brick walls had finally molded me into a submissive, path-of-least-resistance educator. I did as I was told, taught what I was told, in the order and at the pace I was told. Not only had I submitted through the years, but I had also lost confidence in my own ability to think and create meaningful lessons and engaging activities on my own.

The 30 Goals Challenge and the #EdChat Twitter chat sessions had poked around in my subconscious and ignited the few embers barely left burning after all those years. This renewed fiery passion for sharing learning with others had been reawakened, and I found myself at a difficult crossroads. In one direction lay a new path being forged by innovative educators across the country who were dissatisfied with being molded into submission and forced to use lesson plans inadequate to suit the needs of digital age learners. In the other direction lay a well-worn path that led to retirement and the comfort of tenure. This path also came without the risk that the other path held— the risk of stepping up, speaking out, and trying something different, something that wasn't in the pacing guide but was just as relevant and more meaningful to the students I was teaching.

I had a choice to make: stand up, step up, and start beating my head against proverbial brick walls again, or take the last eight years I had as an educator and leisurely stroll into retirement. It may surprise you to know that I initially chose the latter.

Sunshine, Rainbows, and Lollipops

One thing connected educators don't often discuss is the roller-coaster of emotions this process will summon from deep within a person. On one hand, I was excited and energized by what I was learning from others. On the other hand, I was equally filled with feelings of inadequacy and overwhelmed at the thought of stepping outside of the traditional education box. How could *I* possibly do the things I was learning from "rock star" educators? I was no one—a nobody.

One evening, I was feeling particularly overwhelmed after an #EdChat session, not by the chat itself, but by an internal struggle over the direction my life would need to take if I wanted to embrace my new role as a connected educator. There was no longer just *a* path to follow. I knew in my heart that a decision had to be made as to *which* path I would follow.

Later that evening, overcome with emotion, I reached out to several "rock star" educators I had become Twitter friends with over the course of the previous months. With a heavy heart, and tears streaking my cheeks, I wrote each one to thank them for their selflessness in sharing what they were doing in their schools, and for reawakening in me the spark that had lead me to teaching in the first place. I also let them know that I had decided to relish in the joy and inspiration the last few months had brought me, but that I would no longer be joining the Twitter chats. I had decided to ride out the last few years until retirement continuing on the road I had been on before I fell down the connected educator rabbit hole. I explained that, while their work was wonderful, I simply wasn't capable of the doing the same. I, after all, wasn't a rock star teacher.

The next morning, I woke up early to get ready for work, but a persistent voice in the back of my mind told me to check my email. I argued with this nagging voice that there was no need to check my email as it had only been a few hours since I had sent the emails the night before. "Not to mention," I said to the annoying voice, "No one is even going to take the time to read my email, much less respond, because I am a no one—a nobody."

To prove that I was right, I opened my email. To my amazement, my inbox contained emails from *every single person* I had emailed the night before. I read in disbelief. Each email carried a similar message of hope, love, and support, encouraging me to not give up. They told me that I didn't have to be this rock star educator or that superstar teacher; the only thing I ever needed to be was the best *me* I could be, each and every day. They encouraged me to start small, to try just one new thing and see how it went. They also reassured me that if I chose to take this different path, they would have my back the whole journey, and they have.

I knew at that moment my life was about to change. I could no longer look myself in the mirror each day if I didn't at least try this different path. It has been a long, hard, exhausting, sometimes exasperating yet rewarding, thrilling, inspiring, almost intoxicating ride—I hope to never get off.

That, my friends, is why I believe in the power of social media. Just 140 characters at a time transformed my life 180 degrees. Social media has led me down a path that grabbed me, picked me up, and shook up my entire professional and personal life.

Set Yourself up for Success

Know Your Audience

I often joke that school librarians are the bartenders of their schools. Students, teachers, and support staff often saunter up to the circulation desk and share their joys and heartaches with us. We listen, nod our heads, furrow our brows, and smile. Sometimes from across the desk we slide them the perfect book that might give them perspective on their situation, assure them they aren't alone, or offer a much-needed escape from the pressing realities of the world. After all, what happens in the library stays in the library.

Particularly for students who are on the fringe—the marginalized and those who just don't "fit"—school libraries can be a place of refuge: a safe place where they won't be judged or condemned, but instead protected and loved unconditionally.

My co-librarian, Gabriella DuBose, spent a confounding amount of time sitting, chatting, and listening to library visitors. We had books to catalogue, bulletin boards to hang, reading promotions to plan, collaborative lessons to develop; the list went on and on. I didn't understand why she would waste her time socializing when we had so much work to do.

It took a while for me to realize why I needed to channel my inner Gabriella. None of the things I was prioritizing: perfect data in the electronic catalog, shelved books, updated displays (not to mention all the other job tasks of a school librarian) were as important as what Gabriela was doing. None. Let me reiterate: *none* of these things take precedence over building relationships with our patrons. We are a service-oriented profession, and the service we provide is not to books or technology, it is to the people we interact with every day.

Recently, a student needed someone to listen to her pain. She came into the library distraught over the death of her dog, her companion since she was a toddler. I dropped my to-do list for the day and contacted her teachers so they would know where the student was. I sat, listened, and cried with this student, sharing in her her grief. The time I spent with this one student was more valuable than time I could have spent creating a bulletin board or a report. Once we realize that people are our core focus as school librarians, it is much easier to reach our audience through social media, and assist them in making helpful, productive connections of their own.

Just as we teach our students to know their audience when presenting research, essays, or projects, it is important that we take time to consider our audience and purpose when using social media in school and library settings. Different social media platforms serve different audiences (i.e., students, parents, faculty, greater community, other educators), and they deliver information in different ways. We need to make a concerted effort to meet our varied audience where they are, instead of expecting to meet them in the location most convenient to us.

Advertisers have been aware of the critical importance of knowing their audience since the Golden Age of Radio, so it comes as no surprise that advertisers have adapted to the social mediums of the day (television, the internet, and social media) to connect corporate-sponsored products and specific markets. One of the most obvious examples of this is soap operas. Daytime radio programs specifically targeted women. Corporations, mainly soap manufacturers, sponsored the expense of producing television programs by advertising during these shows. These daytime programs, first on the radio and then later on television, became widely known as soap operas (Hiskey, 2010).

While we don't have to sell soap to keep our libraries, we can learn from advertising companies. Telling our stories and sharing information about the variety of services our libraries offer is critical. We must be vigilant in keeping up with the latest trends in technology, especially in the technological fields that deal with communication. Keeping an eye on advertising trends can be a helpful and easy source for insight into the wide demographics of which we must be aware.

Students

When we consider students and social media demographics, we should keep in mind that ages range from thirteen to eighteen in schools, but we shouldn't stop there. Most statistics reported for social media use among this age group are skewed for several reasons.

First, child internet protection laws prohibit the use of social media sites for students under the age of thirteen (Modo Labs, Inc., 2016). That certainly doesn't mean that students younger than thirteen aren't using social media. My sister-in-law set up Facebook accounts for her children when they were still in grade school, and I know many other parents who set up various social network accounts for their grade-school-aged children as well.

Second, students in this demographic, while not reflected in official statistical data, largely prefer to use messaging or anonymous social media sources because they prefer customizable, visual experiences over other forms of social media. Additionally, students "are very cognizant of the misuse of social media," and are "concern[ed] about privacy and security." The "combination of visual and impermanence in a mobile platform is the key to this generation's technology interest (Modo Labs, Inc., 2016)."

Parents

Seventy-nine percent of online adults (ages 18–65+) use Facebook (Greenwood, Perrin, & Duggan, 2016). Given this statistic, it makes sense that one of the first places we share and celebrate student successes is through a school library Facebook page. When my grandson started kindergarten during the 2016–17 school year, one of the first things I did was go to the school's website to see if, and how, they were connected to social media. I then immediately "liked" and turned on notifications for their Facebook page. Currently, the school library utilizes the schoolwide Facebook page. This is a perfectly acceptable start, especially if the person running the page is reliable and posts new library information in a timely fashion.

The win-win of using social media in this manner is that you meet parents in a place that they frequent on a regular basis, and parents see posts from your library in their Facebook newsfeeds. The interaction feels natural, keeps them informed, and makes them feel connected to their child's school while not seeming like another chore they have to do.

Faculty

The way school faculty utilizes social media varies widely. Each school district's technology department grants levels of access to a school's various social media outlets. This is the number one factor that influences what, if any, social media is used by faculty. In a system that understands and embraces the positive impact social media can have on professional learning, parent communication, and community connections—and one that has a more or less open-access technology policy regarding the use of social media—the type of social media used can be traced back to two determiners. The first is modeling of social media use by administration. Teachers look to their administration for guidance because social media is seen by many as a gray area, and teachers do not want to say or do something on social media that would reflect poorly on the school. The second determiner is the age of the faculty members, which can vary widely. Age often determines what type of social media is used. Educators, like most of us, are drawn to what feels most comfortable and what we use in our personal lives.

Community Members

Using social media to reach community members most often requires the use of more than one social media outlet. Those used most frequently by school districts are Facebook and Twitter, which fit with the Pew Research Center study of demographics of usage (2017). Knowing the community member audience and disseminating information about your school through social media takes a concerted effort, so does developing a recognizable brand in the social media realm on behalf of your school or school district.

Other Educators

Social media is a powerful tool for connecting with other educators and growing professionaly through connections made outside of your own school or district. The approach you use depends heavily on the age demographic of the educators involved and what social media they personally feel comfortable using, and thus varies widely.

Future chapters will expand on each of these target audiences and provide tips, strategies, and real-life examples for using social media to expand your reach beyond the school walls to benefit students, teachers, parents, community members, and others.

CHAPTER 2

Secure Buy-In from Administrators and Parents

Convincing administrators and parents to allow social media in our schools often feels like an uphill battle for connected librarians. Administrators are understandably cautious about what, and whom, is allowed access to students, in both the physical and virtual worlds. While their actions may cause frustration, administrators are the protectors of our precious students, and they go to great lengths to ensure student safety; often up late at night with worries and concerns about the students they serve.

District technology coordinators ensure schools are compliant with E-rate requirements, and they manage bandwidth capability to meet the educational needs of the school community. More than that, district technology coordinators are defenders of the virtual gateway, which holds the key to amazing learning opportunities but also to people with nefarious intentions. Guarding this gateway is paramount.

Parents, including myself and my own daughters, are rightfully concerned about strangers who might harm their children, not just on a playground or in another physical location, but through technologies used every day in our homes and through everyday technology we use, like cell phones, tablets, and other smart or connected devices. With these dangers in mind, one would think the best thing we could do is to slam the virtual door shut and not allow students access at all. This approach, however, would leave our children more vulnerable and unprotected to potential threats because they wouldn't have learned how to avoid them and received support for using technology safely.

This chapter will address some of the fears and concerns around social media and propose ways to approach this subject for positive change.

Winning Hearts and Minds

School librarians are in a unique position to partner with administrators and parents and set up parameters for students to navigate social media in an informed manner that can lead to enhanced learning and success.

Future-ready school librarians are educational thought leaders as well as child advocates. Fear and the desire to protect students often prevent administrators from conceptualizing social media as an integral part of our emerging, technology driven educational system. According to the National Education

Technology Plan (NETP), various forms of social media use by students are viewed as not only essential, but commonplace, in today's schools (U.S. Department of Education, 2017). Social media tools give students a voice to communicate with mentors, peers, teachers, subject area experts, and more. Administrators whose vision falls short in imagining the possibilities for social media to enhance and personalize the educational experience for students are ultimately hindering deeper learning. They are also setting students up for failure once they leave the safety of school, and are culpable adults. Students need real-world experiences where they can practice applying their knowledge. It makes them safer because they are prepared and know what to expect.

I recently visited my three-year-old granddaughter. As we walked hand-in-hand to various places, I made sure to talk with her about, and model safety rules for, crossing the road. We put our hands up above our eyes and stood in a searching stance. I scanned the street in an exaggerated fashion and said loudly, "We look both ways before we cross the road. Look to the left. Look to the right. All clear? If yes, let's go. If no, wait. Always be safe."

After she had looked both ways, I asked her if it was safe to cross the road. There are many ways to teach someone a new skill. I could have taught her how to cross the road safely by explaining the process to her, or we could have read a book. She could have colored a picture or watched a video of someone crossing the street. She could have played a video game about street safety. But none of those options would have sufficed. I would have been ill at ease sending her into the world to apply this knowledge without giving her the opportunity to repeatedly practice what I had modeled in real life.

As parents, grandparents, and educators, part of our job is to model how to safely navigate the physical world around us. We don't lock our children in the house only to scoot them out the door when they are legal adults, hoping the life lessons we taught through various simulations will easily and seamlessly transfer to real-life experiences. As adults, we know that practicing in authentic, real-life situations is the best measure of understanding, evidenced by doctors completing residencies, teachers practicums, and others completing some form or other of required practice for their chosen profession.

We can "lock" students out of social media and teach them how to navigate the virtual world through songs, color sheets, books, videos, and online programs or game simulations, but we will fail. Nothing leaves a deeper impact on students than exposure to proper social media usage, modeled daily by respected adults (i.e., parents, teachers, administrators), combined with the opportunity to apply what they've learned in an actual social media space.

Be Informed

To convince the administration that social media belongs in schools, we must be educated about the law. These laws are confusing, and the consequences of misinterpreting them are frightening, which often leads to overly restrictive internet filters. But, if we know exactly what is and is not allowed under the Family Educational Rights and Privacy Act (FERPA), the Children's Internet Protection Act (CIPA), and the Children's Online Privacy Protection Act (COPPA), we can keep our colleagues well informed. For example, I often recommend the interview "Straight from the DOE: Dispelling Myths About Blocked Sites" because I've found the following guidance from DOE Director of Education Technology Karen Cator extremely helpful in navigating social media use in my own school.

- **Accessing YouTube is not violating CIPA rules.** "Absolutely it's not circumventing the rules," Cator says. "The rule is to block inappropriate sites. All sorts of YouTube videos are helpful in explaining complex concepts or telling a story, or for hearing an expert or an authentic voice—they present learning opportunities that are really helpful."

- **Websites don't have to be blocked for teachers.** "Some of the comments I saw online had to do with teachers wondering why they can't access these sites," Cator says. "They absolutely can. There's nothing that says that sites have to be blocked for adults."

- **Broad filters are not helpful.** "What we have had is what I consider brute force technologies that shut down wide swaths of the internet, like all of YouTube, for example. Or they may shut down anything that has anything to do with social media, or anything that is a game," Cator says. "These broad filters aren't actually very helpful, because we need much more nuanced filtering."

- **Schools will not lose E-rate funding by unblocking appropriate sites.** Cator said she's never heard of a school losing E-rate funding due to allowing appropriate sites blocked by filters.

- **Kids need to be taught how to be responsible digital citizens.** "[We need to] address the topic at school or home in the form of education," Cator says. "How do we educate this generation of young people to be safe online, to be secure online, to protect their personal information, to understand privacy, and how that all plays out when they're in an online space?"

- **Teachers should be trusted.** "If the technology fails
  us and filters something appropriate and useful, and
  if teachers in their professional judgment think it's
  appropriate, they should be able to show it," said Cator.
  "Teachers need to impose their professional judgment
  on materials that are available to their students."
  (Barseghian & Cator, 2011)

I have anonymously delivered copies of this interview, with
applicable sections highlighted when I am advocating for
teachers and students to gain access to a particular social media
platform. This approach rarely falls short of changing minds,
but when it does, at least I've made an effort to inform those in
control of the filtering algorithms.

Model, Model, Model

Eric Sheninger's book, *Digital Leadership: Changing Paradigms for
Changing Times*, would make an excellent gift to your administrators on National School Principal's Day or a similar occasion.
Eric's story of transformation from a social media-phobic
administrator to a social media advocate is one every administrator needs to hear. Part of Eric's transformation happened
when he became a connected educator, so another way to inform
our colleagues would be to highlight Connected Educators
Month and use it as a platform to encourage administrators
to get connected. Perhaps the most effective way school librarians can gently nudge administrators and parents toward
understanding the positive power of social media is through
modeling, modeling, modeling.

Modeling involves gaining access to restricted sites at school,
which is no easy feat. What follows is my simple formula for how

to chip away at the fear that encapsulates and paralyzes change from happening in your school district.

1. Have a legitimate lesson that can only be done using only a specific social media tool (i.e., Twitter, Instagram, or Snapchat). This is even more effective if you have collaborated on a lesson with one or more teachers because it shows teacher buy-in already has been established.

2. Present evidence of how this lesson, or a similar lesson using your specific social media tool, has been successfully used by other educators.

3. Ask (plead, beg, bribe with cookies, promise to never ask again—wink, wink, fingers crossed) the district instructional technology director to unblock your specific social media tool just for that one lesson, one period, one block, one day.

4. Once the lesson has been successfully completed: document, document, document! Create a video showing student excitement and engagement. Get student feedback regarding the lesson. Write a blog post about the lesson, with an emphasis on just how vital your specific social media tool was to the success of the lesson. Be sure to sing the praises of the administrator who was forward thinking enough to see the value in using your specific social media tool. Maybe even get the kids to write the administrator thank you notes for granting access to such a fun and engaging lesson.

Manipulative? Maybe. Effective? Yes, but only if the lesson was well orchestrated and the students were truly enthralled. It works much like toppling dominoes—you only have to get the first one started. Students who are blown away by a lesson centered on the use of a favorite social media tool might actually talk to their parents about what they did in school. Imagine the look on a parent's face when they ask their child what they did in school that day and, instead of the rote "nothing," they get a bubbling, over-enthusiastic accounting of the day's lesson instead. The parents, in shock that their child is excited about what they learned in school, tell their friends. Their friends ask their own kids if they did a similar activity. When those parents learn that their child did not participate in a similar activity, they call the school wanting to know why teacher A is using a fun social media tool, but teacher B (their kid's teacher) isn't. Teacher B feels the pressure (as does the administration) and comes to you, the school librarian, and asks you to teach your lesson to their class. Once again, you are off to profusely apologize for asking again, but, could your specific social media tool be unblocked again, just for that one lesson, one period, one block, one day?

Eventually, with enough student and parent pressure, and through your diligent modeling, the administration will begin to see the value of unblocking social media tools so that all students can benefit without jumping through a crazy set of unnecessary hoops each time an educator creates a lesson plan that involves digital citizenship.

Soothing Parents' Frazzled Nerves

Most of the parents we serve have never been formally educated in the academic or professional use of social media. Additionally, parents are unsure of how they can protect their children from the potential hazards of using electronic devices. This is where school librarians can lead the way, by building trusting relationships and calming frazzled nerves.

School librarians are experts at meeting learners where they are, and teaching in the manner each person learns best. Below are a few suggestions for assisting parents in navigating the waters of social media use in BYOD, BYOT, and 1:1 school environments.

- Create newsletters.

- Create step-by-step "how-to" videos.

- Hold in-person, hands-on, Q&A meetings. Be sure to offer morning, afternoon, evening, and weekend sessions, so all parents have the opportunity to attend.

- Partner with your Parent Teacher Association (PTA) or Parent Teacher Organization (PTO).

Topics to cover with parents:

- Connecting your personal Apple ID with your child's school-issued device.

- Setting up parental controls on both personal and school-issued devices.

- Ideas for monitoring child's internet and social media usage.

- Ideas for creating dialogue with your child about cyberbullying.

- Spotting child predators online, and how to protect your children from these threats.

- Accessing various school social media feeds so parents can be more informed of what their children are learning.

- Setting up privacy protections on parents' social media feeds.

- Setting up two-step verifications to protect social media accounts from hackers.

- Spotting fake news and evaluating websites to avoid misinformation in social media feeds.

- How to use the technology their child is using at school.

To put it bluntly, blocking access hurts kids because it leaves a gap in their knowledge. We are educators; it is our job to educate students. Part of that education involves using social media in socially acceptable ways. Sadly, many school districts create this gap in knowledge by putting kids through canned digital citizenship classes and blocking access to social media. They meet the minimum criterion of educating students about the dangers of social media, but they don't meet the real education needs of students. It is short sighted and ineffective policy.

Kids need to see teachers and administrators modeling appropriate use of social media; they need opportunities to explore and practice using social media. Kids need a safe place to fail. The alternative is that *we* fail, and our students aren't adequately educated about social media in tangible ways. We send them into the real world unprepared for, and unprotected from, the consequences that can result from the misuse of social media. We doubly fail our students by denying them access to the the amazing wealth of resources, information, and crucial networking that can be accessed through social media.

CHAPTER 3

Teach Digital Citizenship Using Social Media

Students must both see and practice examples of positive, professional social media use to become competent digital citizens. It is important that school librarians guide students as they create their digital footprints. They can offer insight into many different aspects of the digital landscape—from using a learning management system that offers a "safe" environment for students where they can hone their digital communication skills, to informed discussions about the effects of social media on their personal and professional lives.

Many schools teach digital citizenship by scheduling times for students to visit the library or computer lab to complete canned, online digital citizenship programs. While these programs offer fun, game-like lessons that lead students through various digital citizenship scenarios, they often fail to model any real-world professional use of social media use, and they don't follow up with students to see if they are adhering to the lessons learned. Presented in this manner, digital citizenship simply becomes a curriculum requirement to be checked off a list; it is often taught completely out of context without modeling or opportunities to teach individual students.

Schools also tend to block access to social media sites, even for teachers. Administrators who establish overly-restrictive internet parameters believe that they are doing what is necessary to protect students. Instead, schools that restrict access to social media sites are actually harming students by not teaching, modeling, and assisting students through social media "mistakes" within the safe confines of the school. These schools send students out into a world where people routinely use social media, so proficiency is absolutely expected in a professional setting. Students currently leave public school having little to no experience using social media in an appropriate manner, have rarely seen social media use modeled in a professional environment, and have not had the opportunity to make inevitable mistakes where there are knowledgeable adults who can offer the perspectives of college admissions officers or potential employers.

Modeling Positive Social Media Use

I first really began to understand my role in modeling responsible use of social media when I was working at Hoover High School. My two assistant principals, Jennifer Hogan (@Jennifer_Hogan) and Holly Sutherland (@DrHSutherland), blew me away with the way they harnessed the power of social media for good within a school of over 3,000 high school students. They used a school hashtag and built trusting relationships with students, modeled acceptable ways to use social media, and encouraged students and teachers alike to use the school hashtag to celebrate the amazing learning opportunities, sports events, friendships, and other notable interactions happening at Hoover.

Because the administration and students trusted one another, specifically regarding the use of social media, they could communicate openly. Students knew that they could notify administrators (in person or through private messages) to let them know if other students weren't being responsible with their social media accounts. Rather than punishing the student (or the whole school) for the infraction, the administration could take the opportunity to teach the student one-on-one about the importance of good digital citizenship. That's right, *teach* not *punish*. Jennifer Hogan and Holly Sutherland used these opportunities to discuss, teach, and lead the student to a better understanding of why a certain social media post could reflect poorly on them in the future.

Jennifer and Holly also used social media to stay ahead of trouble within the school. They monitored students' public social media accounts and counted on other students to let them know about anything online of which they might need to be aware. Jennifer and Holly knew when students were upset with each other and a fight might be brewing. They were able to circumvent rising tensions and pull students in to talk (not to confront them about their online posts, but to "see how they were doing"). Often, this was exactly what students needed—someone to listen, someone to care—to deescalate or resolve the situation.

Perhaps one of the best examples of how Jennifer and Holly used social media to model digital citizenship occurred when the Yik Yak app reared its ugly head at Hoover High School. Yik Yak was designed to let people within a five-mile radius post *anything* they wanted, with complete anonymity. Unfortunately, the app was mainly used to bully, taunt, and humiliate. When Yik Yak appeared in our school, the response from administration was quite different from that of most schools. Rather than blocking Yik Yak or shutting down our open policy regarding social media, the administration chose to harness the power of this new app for good. Together with students, teachers, and community members, the administration led a successful campaign to flood Yik Yak in our area with nothing but positive messages; the stream of compliments were about our school, the teachers, the students, and their friends. The app eventually lost its appeal to those using it inappropriately, and the "crisis" was averted—but not before teaching a valuable lesson to students about how social media tools, even those deemed to be "unsavory," can be used for good.

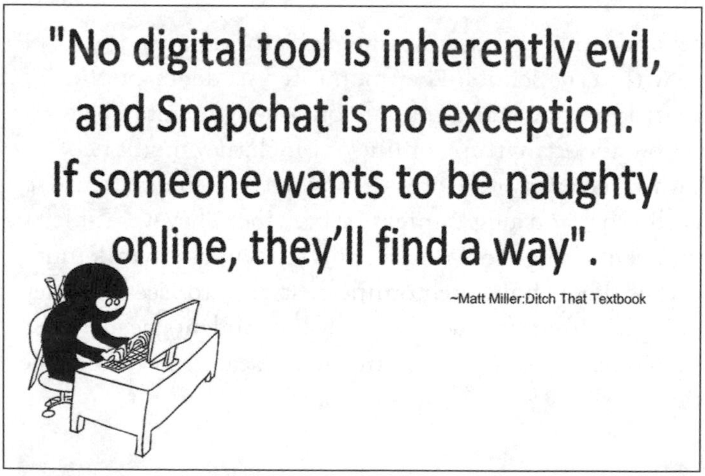

> "No digital tool is inherently evil, and Snapchat is no exception. If someone wants to be naughty online, they'll find a way".
>
> ~Matt Miller:Ditch That Textbook

Figure 3.1 Matt Miller quote.

Matt Miller (@jmattmiller), creator of the blog Ditch That Textbook, sums up my feelings about using social media in school in Figure 3.1.

This statement is true of all social media apps and websites, and it will continue to be true as social media venues change and evolve. I would venture to say that Jennifer Hogan and Holly Sutherland would agree.

School Librarians Leading Change

Daisaku Ikeda, Buddhist philosopher, educator, and author said, "When we change, the world changes. The key to all change is in our inner transformation—a change of our hearts and minds. This is human revolution. We all have the power to change. When we realize this truth, we can bring forth that power anywhere, anytime, and in any situation" (Soka Gakkai International, 2005).

School librarians are poised to help transform opinions about social media, and advocate for policy changes that will ultimately benefit our students. Changing hearts and minds is our "thing." We champion the fight against book banning; it only makes sense that we also use that same tenacity to advocate for students' (and teachers') equitable access to information. Helen Adams, former American Association of School Librarians (AASL) president, addressed the issue in a 2010 AASL blog post: "Many administrators exhibited apprehension of students' on campus use of Web 2.0 interactive tools despite the fact that the skills developed when using social media are necessary for success in a global society" (Adams, 2010).

On the heels of this blog post, and with data gathered from the national Speak Up survey, the AASL launched Banned Websites

Awareness Day. Librarians across the country sponsor events to shine a light on overly restrictive blocking of digital information, including access to social media. I set up an interactive display that connected students directly with our school superintendent's email address so students could write a letter addressing blocking policies that adversely affect their ability to learn. For students who were unsure about how to write an email of this nature, I also provided a template for them to follow. Mine is just one example of how school librarians can champion the cause of intellectual freedom through observing Banned Websites Awareness Day.

Recently, I posed this question on my various social media accounts: Does your school allow students to use social media to practice and develop digital citizenship skills within the safety of the school environment? If so, how?

Sadly, the response was an overwhelming stream of comments like, "my school doesn't allow access to social media for students or teachers" or those that suggested the canned digital citizenship lessons I mentioned earlier (i.e., "we did that"). However, a few great examples emerged.

Rachel Murat (@MrsMurat), an educator from Endwell, New York, shared a student-created "video about digital citizenship and the positive impact that responsible technology use, and social media, have on youth." Students wanted a quick, memorable slogan people could use as a reminder when someone might be using social media inappropriately. "Connect with respect" has become the school's social media mantra. I love that Rachel's school not only allows students to access social media to further their educational pursuits, but the school also gave students a voice through the creation of this video.

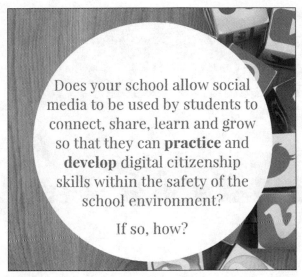

Does your school allow social media to be used by students to connect, share, learn and grow so that they can **practice** and **develop** digital citizenship skills within the safety of the school environment?

If so, how?

Figure 3.2 Student use of social media in schools.

Jennifer Woodruff Brower, an innovation and media services specialist at Whitley County Consolidated Schools in Indiana, shared that the new tech high school does a mock election each year. Students create their own parties and set up associated social media accounts. Students have strict guidelines to never mention or tag the school, the school district, or where they are located in order to protect their privacy. This exercise gets students involved with politically minded tweets and other social media venues with guidance from teachers.

Eric Neuman (@EricNeuman), a New York City school librarian, shared an idea he got from his colleague, Marilyn Arnone, Ph.D. Depending on the administration in charge, he promotes the library book club using group-specific hashtags. Eric also allows his students to take pictures with his school-issued iPad and post them to the library's Twitter and Instagram accounts (after his approval). Eric's example is a great way, especially for those

Figure 3.3 Connect with respect.

who teach students younger than thirteen, for students to gain real-world experience using social media responsibly and for an educational purpose.

Ideas for Using Social Media to Teach Digital Citizenship

The following are just a few ideas for using social media tools in the library or classroom. These activities require students to share information and communicate publicly, making the perfect opportunities to model and practice positive digital citizenship. It's no coincidence the activities are also highly motviating and engaging—students love the opportunity to be creators, give and receive comments, and see their activities published in real time.

Story Features

SnapChat, Instagram, and Facebook all now have "stories" features. Story features allow users to create a continuous flow of images and videos that together weave a story of a particular day or event. Kids love taking selfies, and being able to add crazy filters, stickers, and text makes it even more fun! Why not use these features with students? Here are a few ideas to get you started, but let your imagination run wild.

- Either you or your students can create vocabulary stories by taking pictures of images that represent a word. Use the text feature to add the vocabulary word and definition to the image.

- Challenge students to create stories that include real-world examples of math, science, social studies, grammar, or other subjects. You can also create stories to help students conceptualize the real-world relevance of what they are learning.

- Create a Snapchat story to help your students study for an upcoming exam. Add the top ten most important things to remember for a quiz or test as snaps in your story. Students can watch your story, and it becomes an instant study session.

Matt Miller of Ditch That Textbook suggests, "Do a student take-over—let students take over the school/district social media accounts! After some clear expectations and ground rules, students can be very creative and give a fresh perspective to student life (Miller, 2017)." What better way to teach digital citizenship than to give students some guided on-the-job training?

Contests

Contests can be highly engaging and motivating for students, and there is no better platform than social media. The mobile technology company Crescerance offers the following suggestions for using Snapchat to engage with students:

- **Selfie Spirit!** During homecoming season, most high schools celebrate with Spirit Day. Snap us a selfie in your Falcon's best. The selfie that exemplifies the most Falcon pride wins a prize. Bring in a community partner to sponsor the contest and giveaway the prize.

- **Have a Snapenger Hunt.** You can focus this around a more educational topic like Earth Day. Make a list of items related to earth day and protecting the environment. You can even have students define what the object is with a caption. The first student to find and snap all the items wins a prize. Leveraging community resources works here as well. (2015)

Aren't "Canned" Online Digital Citizenship Sessions Worthwhile?

It might seem that I am against online digital citizenship passports, sessions, videos, workshops, and simulations because I refer to them as "canned." These online digital citizenship resources do have a purpose and they can all help to get the digital citizenship conversation started in your school. However, they should not be the whole kit and kaboodle, BAM—we're done, kind of lesson I hear about all too often. They must be incorporated into the fabric of our lessons, and into the social fabric of our libraries.

What if teaching our students about online digital safety and digital citizenship was like teaching someone to be a tightrope walker or a flying trapeze artist? In the majority of our schools, students learning to walk a tightrope or fly through the air on a trapeze would review, watch videos, and answer questions in guided online simulations. Students would go through a series of these simulations once during their school career, or even every year until they graduated. Upon leaving our school system, students would be expected to, based on the online training they received, perform a high-wire and flying trapeze act before a live audience without a safety net. How confident would you be that your students, trained with nothing more than online simulations, would be able to successfully perform?

To truly understand digital citizenship, students must have opportunities to repeatedly practice in real-world, student-centered environments. It is only through practice, making and learning from mistakes, that students will be prepared to put forth a positive digital footprint that reflects the best they have to offer the world when they leave the safety of our schools.

DIGITAL CITIZENSHIP RESOURCES

Common Sense Media (commonsensemedia.org)

BrainPop and BrainPop Jr. (brainpop.com)

Net Safe (planetnutshell.com/netsafe)

NetSmartzKids (netsmartkidz.org)

Common Craft (commoncraft.com)

On Guard Online (onguardonline.gov)

Stop Bullying (stopbullying.gov)

CHAPTER 4

Anonymity and Social Media

With the rise of anonymous social media sites and apps, students (and adults) are under the misguided impression that what they say and do online is, and always will be, private. This is not the case. School librarians can model acceptable use so that students have a solid understanding of how they may be expected to use social media once they are career based.

Social Media Is Not a Mask

Did you know that not everyone on social media is who they say they are? To many, social media sites are places where they can put on different masks or personas and pretend to be someone else for a while. Students (and adults) are led into a false sense of anonymity while online that, sadly, leads to saying things they would never utter in face-to-face conversations. Let's face it, there is no such thing as privacy or complete anonymity anymore, especially if you use the internet. I have a friend whose son is so afraid of the government spying on him that he lives in an "off-the-grid" community. The funny thing is that the government scrutinizes her son's community more closely than they do ordinary citizens. Regardless, the assumption of privacy—and certainly complete anonymity—in the world of social media is an oxymoron.

Yik Yak and Other Anonymous Apps

Certain online messaging apps, like the now-defunct Yik Yak, gave users the ability to send anonymous messages to, and about, others within a five-mile radius of the user's location. In schools these apps quickly became known for cyberbullying. Wondering where students get their fix for posting anonymous random (or not so random) thoughts now that Yik Yak is gone? Never fear, other apps are there! Jodel, Whisper, Candid, After School, and ASKfm are the top contenders for this social media niche (Gangwar, 2017).

In a recent online post for Lifewire, a website that offers advice on how to get the most out of technology, Elise Moreau surmised that social media status updates have become a bit overwhelming, especially for school-aged kids. She goes on to state that this pressure from social media has actually led to the rise in anonymous apps, which allow posters to feel a bit less scrutinized, and free to express their true feelings rather than what is expected from social media posts on sites like Instagram (Moreau, 2017).

How should school librarians engage with anonymous apps? Do we model appropriate use of these apps and, if so, how would anyone know who we were online? Perhaps the best thing we can do is to be aware of the existence of anonymous apps, take every opportunity that presents itself to remind students that *anonymous* doesn't really mean *anonymous*, and, if need be, create projects that combat the negativity so often associated with anonymous apps. (I'm thinking of the project I mentioned in Chapter 3; Jennifer Hogan and Holly Sutherland flooded the Yik Yak app with positivity when it hit the Hoover High School campus.)

Snapchat

While not an anonymous site, Snapchat is often viewed as such by students because the "snaps"—images, texts, and videos sent through Snapchat—all "disappear." Snaps can be set to be viewed for one to ten seconds, after which time they vanish and, in theory, cannot be viewed again. In reality, screenshots of apps are easily taken, and a person can always record your snaps with another device. There is no failsafe way to delete your snaps, tweets, or other social media posts online; it is almost always possible to retrieve them after they have been deleted.

When I use Snapchat in the school library, I like to save my snaps to my phone's camera roll before adding them to the story I am building for the day. This way, I can also easily share these

Figure 4.1 Social media poster created for James Clemens High School (JCHS).

same snaps on my other school library social media sites. In fact, I put together an end-of-the-year video using images and video that were originally taken with the Snapchat app. You can view it online at youtube.com/watch?v=TZl3TxsOf2E.

Twitter and Facebook

Recently, Twitter and Facebook have started cracking down on people creating anonymous accounts, insisting that people must associate their real names with their accounts, but there are certainly ways around these new rules. I have one friend who has three separate Facebook accounts: one that her employer knows about; one that her family knows about; and one that her friends know about. Our students do the same thing with the social media apps they are using, *especially* if their parents monitor their social media use.

As my friend did, students want some anonymity and independence. While presenting a Twitter 101 session at a school library conference, I had an attendee ask if she could create more than one Twitter account. I replied that she could, and I highly recommended creating a personal account and a separate school account. School librarians and other education professionals can use their school account to celebrate and document the learning taking place in their school (Figure 4.1). They can use their personal accounts to connect with other educators and grow their PLNs.

The session attendee responded, *in front of everyone,* that she wanted an account where no one would know she was tweeting because she wanted to fuss about things that made her angry. Sigh. I understand that need a place to vent without judgement, but social media just isn't the place. Screaming into a pillow, going for a long walk, leaning on a friend who can relate—all are better ways to get out the frustrations we experience in even the best of jobs. Personally, I have learned that focusing on the negative only allows that negativity to spawn and grow. Thus, I choose to refocus my train of thought when negative feelings creep in. I suggested to the session attendee that it was certainly possible to use an anonymous Twitter account to vent, but that her time and effort might be better spent in other ways. Helping our students learn to refocus their energies in positive ways rather than feeding negative energy is a life skill that will serve them—and us—well.

For Facebook, I recommend a similar prescription as I do for Twitter: separate accounts for personal and school use. I also use my personal Facebook account for posting things like my grandchildren, pets, and delicious food I'm eating. I try to avoid posting anything negative because I strongly believe that the type of energy you put into the world, positive or negative, is the energy you will receive from the world. As for Twitter, my personal account is used almost exclusively for professional growth and development, and I always post with positive vibes of support and collaboration.

Social Media Displays

Social media displays are similar to other library displays—such as book displays, monthly theme displays, and reading promotion displays—only they involve social media.

The benefit of using social media displays is that they can:

- help connect students, teachers, administrators, and parents to the school library's social media accounts;

- encourage two-way interaction with the library;

- allow students a place learn how to use social media in an educationally (and professionally) acceptable manner;

- empower student voice; and

- allow the librarian and others to share the story of the library's role in the day-to-day operation of the school.

I do not believe that school librarians should be advocating for the use of anonymous or "temporary" social media sites like Whisper or Snapchat, but I do think it is important to keep the lines of communication open with our students. We need to address the social media apps they are using in a way that doesn't alienate our students. Additionally, we need to know about, and meet, students where they are, which is one reason I have used Snapchat when working in a high school library (Figure 4.2).

Figure 4.2 James Clemens High School (JCHS) Snapchat icon.

Whisper Display Idea

If you know that your students are using a particular anonymous app, you should use these trends to your advantage. For example, I knew that some of my high school students liked using the Whisper app. This app appeals to the students I spoke with because they can confess thoughts that are emotionally heavy without anyone knowing the thoughts are theirs. While I don't have a Whisper account for myself or for the school library, that doesn't mean students can't be encouraged to use it for learning.

A fun library display might feature "whispers" from book characters. Students could create whispers for their favorite book characters, or make a contest out of guessing which characters posted which anonymous whisper. The contest to match characters with whispers may seem a bit backward for an anonymous app display, but this type of activity shows students how simple it is to match the whisper with the person, particularly when you know the person. The upside? No lecturing or preaching!

Snapchat Display Ideas

In my high school library, Snapchat wasn't ever just a special display. Rather, I used Snapchat as a way to make our library displays interactive and to elicit student involvement in our monthly or weekly library celebrations. For Banned Books Week and Banned Website Awareness Day, I used Snapchat as a feature that students could use to voice their opinions about apps and websites that they felt they needed access to at school (see Figure 4.3). This not only got students using their social media to advocate for a cause, but also strengthened their persuasive writing and thinking skills. For Poem in Your Pocket Day and National Poetry Month, students were encouraged to explore various forms of poetry, and to submit original works of their own (see Figures 4.4 and 4.5). Snapchat codes were used to lead students to more information on the topic.

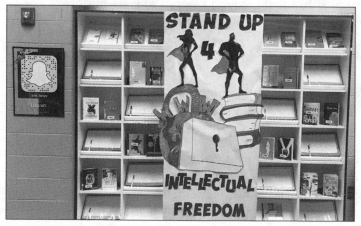

Figure 4.3 Intellectual freedom poster integrating Snapchat.

Figure 4.4 Poem in Your Pocket display.

Figure 4.5 National Poetry Month display.

These types of displays, as well as new books, exciting maker-space activities, and more were all shared with students on a daily basis through the school library Snapchat account. In fact, once word got around about the library Snapchat account, I would often have students calling me over to ask if I would take and post a snap of what they had created in the makerspace, or of the book they were reading, or of them hanging out with friends in the library.

With regard to anonymous apps and websites, the most important thing school librarians can do is to hold open the doors of communication for our students, model proper use for apps and websites prevalent in your school, and provide guidance about online safety and responsibility whenever, and however, possible.

PART TWO

Harness the Power of Social Media Tools for Learning

CHAPTER 5

Blogs and Digital Portfolios

B logging and building personal digital portfolios give students ownership over their own digital footprints and give real-world relevance to learning and practicing good digital citizenship. Blogs and digital portfolios are places for students (and teachers) to showcase growth and reflection over the course of their school career. Think of a digital portfolio as a living, breathing conglomeration—of text, electronic files, images, multimedia, blog entries, hyperlinks, and more—that grows, changes, and transforms as the individual does.

Student Digital Portfolios

If students are going to be competitive in an ever-growing, global competition for college admittance, scholarships, and employment opportunities, they must maintain digital portfolios (with, or without blog components). In fact, in 2015, eighty of the country's most selective institutions—including the Ivy League schools, Stanford, University of Chicago, Amherst, Swarthmore, and Williams—announced a plan to offer free ePortfolios (digital portfolios) to high school students. Students "[would] be encouraged to upload examples of their best work, starting in ninth grade, to provide colleges and universities with more and better information about their capabilities and potential" (Craig, 2015).

Daniel Whitt (@WhittMister), a coordinator of instructional technology for Madison city schools, describes why digital portfolios are so important today in his film "Digital Portfolios: The Whole Child, The Whole Story" (watch the trailer at youtu.be/uUsy2ORFqII). The film reveals how we get so distracted by the academics that we sometimes fail to see all the other talents a student possesses. Portfolios can showcase entirely different dimensions of a student, and they offer insight to the personal genius we may have otherwise dismissed as "not very good in school." A transcript shows letters and numbers. A digital portfolio shows knowledge and achievement.

Employers are also taking note of digital portfolios. My own daughter has suffered from the lack of a digital portfolio; it has affected her ability to find a job in her field. Her experience of applying for a job in her degree field often started with the potential employer asking for a link to her digital portfolio. I suspect many others encounter this as well. Employers know that you paid tuition and sat through classes long enough to earn a degree, but they really want to evaluate the quality of work you can contribute to their company. This isn't translated by a grade point average or a traditional resume; a digital portfolio demonstrates your skills, abilities, and achievements as they relate to the position you are seeking.

What Should Go in a Digital Portfolio?

Daniel Whitt was gracious enough to share all of his digital portfolio files for Grades 3–12 on the Madison City School website. Sean Neal's digital portfolio (seanneal.weebly.com) is one of my favorites to use when teaching my high school students about building their own. The first thing you see on Sean's digital portfolio is an image of musical notes. I use this to lead a discussion about the importance of images and the messages they convey to a person viewing your site. Naturally, this leads to a discussion of creating a positive digital footprint on social media sites, as well as respecting copyright by knowing how and where to locate quality and free-to-use images (such as those found on CreativeCommons.org). I also encourage students to elicit the help of students in our photography courses and photography club to get personalized photos, rather than using stock photos from the internet. This personal touch goes a long way to endear the subject to the portfolio viewers.

About Me

The next item we review on Sean's digital portfolio is his About Me information. Sean has this information on his portfolio's landing page. Although students have the option to design their spaces in a way that reflects their own personalities, an About

Me section is a must; it is the student's "elevator speech" to the world about who they are. Writing the About Me section of the digital portfolio is perhaps one of the most difficult tasks for both students and teachers. It has been ingrained in us to be humble, and writing an About Me profile feels a bit like bragging. This portion of a digital portfolio isn't bragging; it's putting your best foot forward in the form of a written introduction , and it's one of the first impressions you'll make on a college scholarship board or future employer.

At this point in my lesson, I let students brainstorm what pages and tabs they want to build into their digital portfolios. A page or tab covering academics is required, so that students can monitor the academic work they feel best represents their efforts. I also encourage students to add pages or tabs that show who they are beyond academics. If they are on a sports team, in the band, part of a club, or do volunteer work, students are encouraged to include this information to tell their "whole story."

I make it a point to tell students how their portfolio will change over time as they themselves change, grow, learn, and go through new life experiences. I also show them the professional digital portfolio that I maintain. Curating a digital portfolio is a lifelong endeavor that requires one to critically assess and evaluate their progress and achievements.

Documents and Sample Work

I always recommend students add a page or tab to their digital portfolio for professional letters of recommendation, cover letters, resumes, and other documents that potential employers may request. Year after year, I see students freaking out as they search through emails and computer files, hunting for the elusive letter of recommendation they had saved . . . somewhere.

By creating a space for these critical documents within their digital portfolios, students can stress about more important things than the location of a document. One does need to keep in mind, however, that documents of this nature can contain sensitive personal information that one would not want to share publicly. I show students how certain pages and tabs can be password-protected to ensure their privacy.

This part of my lesson lends itself to starting a conversation about online safety and ways that predators can manipulate and pull personal information from unsuspecting students. We all want to think we would never fall for such a thing, talking candidly about common methods and tricks of those who mean harm will, while not always acknowledged, leave a lasting impression on students. It is my hope that this information will be helpful if students are ever confronted with an undesirable online encounter.

Blog Component

Blog components are the last element we discuss adding to student digital portfolios. Students may wish to keep their blog components completely private. I like to think of this as a space where students can use writing to sort out their thoughts, ideas, dreams, and expectations of the world. Did they hear a great song that they just want to talk about? Was there a TV show that struck a personal chord, and they want to get their feelings out in a safe space? Is there something happening in the political arena that has stirred their emotions? A blog offers an excellent place for students to sort through the complexities of the world around them. Ultimately, this builds not only writing skills, but it enables students to examine and reflect on their own emotional growth and understanding of this beautiful thing we call life.

Lastly, I like to highlight the value that colleges and universities place on digital portfolios. Both Georgia Institute of Technology and the University of Georgia offer digital portfolio immersion classes designed "to develop digital portfolios to optimize college applications" (iFolio, 2016). Details from the program include:

- How to stand out to college admissions

- Communicating your strengths

- Planning your digital portfolio

- Your profile and academics

- Activities, service, work experience

- Professional head shot photos

- Media grid and media options

As an Auburn football fan, I would be remiss if I didn't also mention that Auburn University has a stellar ePortfolio site for students (wp.auburn.edu/writing/eportfolio-project). The site is one I often use as an example, especially if teaching digital portfolios during college football season. Check your local and state colleges and universities to see what resources they offer in the development of student digital portfolios. You may be surprised at the resources these institutions are willing to share.

Digital Portfolio Building Tools

Depending on the grade level, your expertise (or lack thereof) with website building, and other factors, there are a variety of tools students can use to get started building their digital portfolios. In my school district, we use the free versions of

Wix or Weebly for their ease of use. These sites easily register students through their school Google accounts, thus keeping schools in line with child internet safety laws. Students who are computer savvy and want to use websites that use HTML or other computer design languages are free to use the website builder that best suits their personal needs and preferences. After students graduate, sites created using a school Google account can be transferred to their personal email accounts.

The Coalition for Access, Affordability and Success, a coalition of more than eighty top-tier colleges and universities, created a free "digital locker" space for students. The space is available to students beginning in the ninth grade. The program's goals are to improve the traditional college application process, which often leaves lower income students at a disadvantage for admission to top-tier colleges.

For students in kindergarten through second grade, a classroom digital portfolio is recommended. My grandson's school has chosen to use the portfolio builder SeeSaw (web.seesaw.me), which can be viewed on any internet-connected device. Common Sense Education has a list of top picks for student portfolio apps and websites that schools should carefully and thoroughly review before beginning a student digital portfolio initiative. You can review this list at www.commonsense.org/education/top-picks/student-portfolio-apps-and-websites. By building digital portfolios in the earliest grades, teachers model and teach reflection of one's own learning progress in a way that teaches the concept of digital citizenship as just being an all-around good citizen, whether in the real world or the virtual one.

All these activities set students on a course to build an authentic digital footprint, and to pay attention to their role as a conscientious digital citizen in a way that goes far beyond watching a few videos or simulations in an online digital citizenship course.

Teacher Digital Portfolios

With the argument for student digital portfolios in mind, let's address reasons why teachers also benefit from creating digital portfolios. As student teachers, one of the most detested tasks was writing reflections; it seemed we were reflecting ad nauseam. These reflections, so vilified in college, become a thing of the past once we found ourselves graduated, certified, and in a classroom or library of our own. As a result, we stopped reflecting on our professional practice.

We tell our students a digital portfolio is a living, growing, constantly changing document that will follow them for the rest of their lives. Educators need to embrace the development and maintenance of digital portfolios as well, but for different reasons than those of students. Educators should be encouraged to maintain a digital portfolio because it serves as a tool for continued professional reflection. Personally, I prefer to use the blog portion of my digital portfolio for these reflections, and they have turned out to be quite helpful throughout the years.

Blogging was another goal I chose to pursue back in 2010, when I discovered Shelly Terrell's 30 Goals Challenge. When I first considered writing a blog as one of my challenges, my thoughts ran wild: *I'm not a writer. How am I going to find the time to write a blog? I don't really have anything new or of any value to write in a blog. No one will even read my blog.*

What I have since realized is that none of my fears mattered because blogging isn't about any of those things; it's about reflecting for *myself.* While I know and admire many bloggers who write opinion posts, or posts to educate and provide professional development, I have mostly stuck to writing about what happens in my school library: the activities, the students, the collaborative lessons, and so much more. Not only is my blog a reflection of the daily activities in the school library, it is a celebration of the student and teacher learning that can be accredited to interactions with the school library program. It also serves as my own personal reference tool, as I can easily look back at previous years to see what I did for a particular AASL activity, like World Read Aloud Day or Poem in Your Pocket Day, when planning for these same events in the current year.

One year, I made it my goal to write a blog post at the end of each week. I was always be surprised when I sat down to write. I thought to myself, "Geez. This blog post is going to be short. I really didn't do much this week." But when I flipped back through my calendar, I was floored by just how much had actually been accomplished. Writing a weekly blog post of library activities helps to bring a whole new perspective to just how much we do in our schools.

Another bonus to using the blog component of a digital portfolio is that it provides easy, stress-free access to evidence of instructional practice that many school districts require as part of their teacher evaluation system. Instead of scrambling to write a narrative after being reminded of a firm deadline, I can simply provide a link to my digital portfolio, where I have been continually collecting evidence of my professional practice throughout the school year.

Digital portfolios provide a place for students and teachers to showcase the best of who they are through self-evaluation, reflection, and providing evidence in various formats of lifelong learning.

Students should also be encouraged to blog, whether on their own as a component of their digital portfolio or as a part of teaching the grammar and the writing process. Getting students to write blog posts doesn't need to be yet another thing teachers must address in their curriculum and pacing guides. Rather, blogging, even in the early elementary years, is a great way to have students practice writing and grammar in context with something they actually care about.

When I worked as an instructional technology facilitator in a 1:1 school, I helped third- and fourth-grade teachers find ways to connect the 1:1 devices to their curriculum, to enhance learning and instruction. Students had weekly writing prompts that they wrote as part of the curricular requirements. I took these student writings, turned them into blog posts, and shared them with my PLN on Twitter using the hashtag #Comments4Kids (comments4kids.blogspot.com/p/how-to-use-hashtag.html). The hashtag #Comments4Kids is used by students and teachers to find blogs to comment on, and to get comments on their own posts. The first time I posted these writings was right before Thanksgiving break. Third-grade students had written descriptive paragraphs about their favorite holiday desserts. I posted these paragraphs to our third-grade blog and solicited comments using the #Comments4Kids hashtag. When students returned from the break, they were thrilled to see that people from all over the world had read and commented on their writings. In fact, students were begging their teacher, "When can we write some more?!" Students were eager to improve their writing skills, and they put more thought into their writing assignments because they wanted their writing to be included in the next blog post. Thus, writing and grammar, rather than simply being simply a standard to be learned, became a skill that had real-world relevance beyond the classroom, which inspired students to actively learn and improve.

CHAPTER 6

The Magic of Hashtags

Hashtags, short words or phrases preceded by the pound sign (#), first started being widely used by Twitter in 2009. Today, hashtags are no longer limited to the realm of social media, but they have changed how we view our favorite television shows, sporting events, and even the news. Through the magic of hashtags, we can connect with people around the world to discuss a common topic. Our students no longer passively watch television; they actively engage with other viewers and share commentary on a variety of topics. Students are becoming acutely aware of the power of their own voice. School librarians should be well versed in the power of social media and how hashtags can be leveraged in the educational arena and as a powerful tool for professional growth.

The three most popular social media websites utilizing the magic of hashtags are Facebook, Instagram, and Twitter. Hashtags can be used to fine tune a string of comments, and turn them into a synchronized conversation regarding a common topic or theme. Marketing and money are the driving factors behind most hashtags we see in our daily lives. For schools and educators, however, hashtags can contribute to building a positive school or district brand, build connections between classrooms and parents, build PLNs, celebrate student learning, and so much more.

Facebook Hashtags

Facebook, while the "oldest" social media platform of the three we will discuss, was among the last to embrace the use of hashtags. Thus, hashtags don't carry quite the same magic on Facebook as they do on other social media websites. I prefer using Facebook for my personal life, sharing pictures of my cats and dog, my grandchildren, what I eat, and pretty much the same mundane things everyone else shares. For professional use, Facebook Groups currently reign supreme over searching hashtags, at least in this context. Here are my current favorite Facebook groups:

- Future Ready Librarians (facebook.com/groups/ futurereadylibrarians)

- The School Librarian's Workshop (facebook.com/ groups/57409801076/)

- MakerSpaces and the Participatory Library (facebook. com/groups/librarymaker/)

Hashtags on Facebook *do* help to locate existing Facebook groups for topics of professional interest. For example, typing #makerspace into the search bar on Facebook will yield a variety of results categorized into these sections: Top, Latest, People, Photos, Videos, Shop, Pages, Places, Groups, Apps, and Events. If you don't find a group for your professional topic, do what Kristen Mattson, Ph.D. (@DrKMattson) did when presenting at a conference about future-ready librarians. Conference attendees wanted to know how they could stay connected with one another so they could continue to connect and share information. On the spot, Mattson searched to see if a Facebook group already existed; seeing that one did not, she created the group for her conference attendees. This group has grown to encompass over 4,000 members nationwide. The one thing we can't be afraid to do is to take the lead and create what we need if it doesn't currently exist. Chances are, if it is something you need, it is most likely something others need as well.

Instagram Hashtags

Instagram is a social media site that allows users to share pictures and videos with followers, either publicly or privately with followers. My favorite thing about Instagram is the ability to post to multiple social media sites like Facebook and Twitter, saving a busy librarian valuable time while providing a big social media boost! I have to admit that I do not use Instagram personally, although I know that my students do. To capture that student audience, I use Instagram to promote and celebrate all the cool things that are happening in our library. When posting to Instagram, I use hashtags associated with my school, district, and library groups I am familiar with, including #TLChat, #makerspace, #futurereadylibs, #ISTElib, #tlelem,

#edchat, #satchat, #GAFE4Littles, #Commetns4Kids, and so many more depending on the nature of the Instagram post.

Hashtags can also be used to search for top posts, people, tags, and places like they are in Facebook. Emily Liscom (@emilyliscom), an elementary school teacher and Instagram expert, in collaboration with the Primary Teacher Collaboration Facebook group, has come up with a smattering of popular hashtags that teachers use on Instagram. A selection of these hashtags appears below.

#teachersfollowteachers	#kindergartenteacher
#teachersofig	#firstgradeteacher
#teachersofinstagram	#secondgradeteacher
#teacherspayteachers	#iteachtoo
#iteachk	#organizedteacher
#iteachfirst	#teacherproblems
#iteachsecond	#teacherhumor
#iteach	#teachersbelike
#teachinginspiration	#classroomorganization
#teachingquotes	#teacher
#classroommanagement	#teachers
#guidedreading	

So what Instagram hashtags can school librarians use? Molly Wetta (@molly_wetta), librarian and manager of The Hub (a teen collections blog for the Young Adult Library Services Association [YALSA]), suggests looking at the hashtag #books-tagram. Molly says that she uses Instagram to highlight recent acquisitions, or to share titles that she is currently reading. She encourages librarians to, "Get creative and take inspiration from other book lovers' accounts—and don't be afraid to highlight music, movies, video games, and more" (Wetta, 2016).

Gwyneth Jones (@GwynethJones), also known as The Daring Librarian (thedaringlibrarian.com), suggests using Instagram to promote your library and literacy. Both still photos and the video component in Instagram provide school librarians (and their students) lots of fun, engaging opportunities to promote what they are reading. From #shelfies to mini book trailers to book reviews, the list of ideas for using Instagram in your school library is endless and limited only by your imagination. And since my imagination often hits a brick wall, I am grateful for the school librarians who share their ideas on Instagram (Jones, 2017).

Below are some suggested hashtags for school librarians. Don't forget to create your own hashtag for your own school library.

#bookfacefriday	#teenlibrarian
#caughtreading	#bookstagram
#shelfies	#librarylife
#bookquotes	#booklover
#librariesofinstagram	#newbooks
#bookdroplife	#bannedbookweek
#highschoollibrary	#booktalk
#schoollibrary	#bookreview

To find other hashtags, go to the search bar in Instagram and start typing a word preceded by the # symbol. A list of hashtags, and how many posts have used each hashtag, will pop up as you type (see Figure 6.1). This will help you to maximize exposure of your posts by using highly followed hashtags.

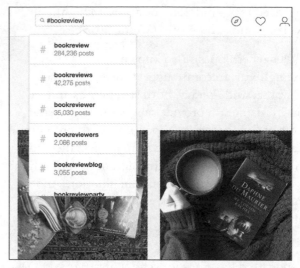

Figure 6.1 Instagram search.

Overall, Instagram is a quick, visually stimulating social media site for finding information about new books, cool displays, makerspace ideas, and other library related topics. Instagram is also the second most used social media site used among students. It is the perfect venue to celebrate students and all things school- and library-related.

Twitter

Hashtags are the key to unlocking the magic of Twitter. I once attended a school library conference and sat in on a session about using Twitter to connect and learn. I excitedly created a Twitter account and then, after letting it sit idle for some time, wondered why nothing was happening. I stumbled upon Shelly Terrell's 30 Goals Challenge and through participating in the challenge was introduced to the #EdChat hashtag. After several #EdChat Twitter chat sessions, the lights turned on for me as I realized hashtags helped to make sense of the "noise" on Twitter. What I refer to as the "noise" is found on the home stream in Twitter. The home stream shows you what every single person you are following is tweeting. If you are following 500 people on Twitter, your home stream will reflect tweets from 500 different people about 500 different topics. Imagine you were in a room with all these people, and they were all talking to you at the same time. Crazy, right? Hashtags quiet that noise into one focused stream of common thought. For example, the #EdChat hashtag narrows the conversation to education-related topics. During the #EdChat Twitter chat sessions, the conversation is further narrowed to one specific educational topic. Twitter is my all-time, number one, favorite social media tool I use when I really want to connect with other educators around the globe. Specifically, Twitter chats leave me renewed and energized, filled with great ideas to take back to my school and valuable connections with other educators.

I like to assist my teachers in finding hashtags suited to their professional interests. Often, I will tweet about a really impressive lesson and include the teacher's Twitter handle and a hashtag specific to their professional teaching field. For instance, Ms. Walker, a third-grade teacher, started using Google Classroom with her students. She focused on using the tool's ability to provide formative assessment throughout the writing process with her students. I watched as, week after week, she led her students to more writing challenges and witnessed their writing bloom with her guidance and use of Google tools. I took the student work—descriptive paragraphs about their favorite Thanksgiving desserts—and made a student blog post out of it. I shared the blog post using several different hashtags to reach several different educational communities. Providing a real-world platform is an excellent way to celebrate students' hard work and elevates their efforts beyond a simple grade.

I use the #Comments4Kids hashtag when I want to get feedback from other teachers and students about student work. I also make sure to return the favor by providing feedback as well for other educators tweeting with the #Comments4Kids hashtag.

I used the #3rdChat hashtag to increase readership of the students' discriptive paragraphs, but I was also modeling hashtag use and building a PLN for Ms. Walker. The hashtag #3rdChat is where third-grade teachers across the country connect to share lessons, celebrate their students, ask for ideas to spice up outdated lessons, and more.

I also used the hashtag #tlchat to share (and model!) how school librarians can assist teachers with student blogging. The responses from teachers and students around the world to her students' descriptive writing was the thing that made Ms. Walker realize the power of Twitter and hashtags; it convinced other teachers in the school as well. When students were read the comments on their blog post, and responses on Twitter, they were jumping out of their skin, asking Ms. Walker when they could write again. The fact that someone who wasn't their teacher, someone outside of their school, found worth in their writing made them want to not only write more, but to write better.

When I first started using Twitter, the only educational hashtag, to my knowledge, was #EdChat. Within a few years, educators started creating hashtags to focus the #EdChat Twitter stream into smaller streams suited to their specific educational interests. #TLChat was created by Joyce Valenza to bring a Twitter chat experience to teacher-librarians exclusively about teacher-librarians. After a year or so, more specific Twitter chats began emerging with hashtags for teacher-liibrarians in different states in different grade levels. Some of the most active librarian hashtags as of this writing include #tlchat (teacher-librarian Chat), #futurereadylibs (part of the Future Ready Initiative), and #ISTELib (part of the ISTE librarians' network). Individual state chats specifically geared toward school librarians in those state currently include these hashtags:

#AISLEChat	#NDLibChat
#ArkTLChat	#NJLibChat
#califlibchat	#SCHSDSLP
#FAMEChat	#TASLChat
#KyLChat	#TxlChat
#MNITEM	#VASLChat
#MWLibChat	

Don't forget to also follow state library conference hashtags. Even if you can't attend the conference in person, you can still learn, and you can gather amazing resources as those in attendance tweet about what they are learning. I was fortunate enough to attend in person and tweet with #TxLA17 and #TxLA17tc in 2017.

I encourage all school librarians to actively participate in their state education chats, as well as those geared toward school librarians. State education chats like #ALEdChat (Alabama ed chat) are where administrators often hang out. We need to be present and make our voices heard in an arena where administrators and decision makers can see that school librarians have valid, informed, competent voices to add to the conversation, and that we are an invaluable resource for schools. Often in these state education Twitter chats, administrators are seeking advice or solutions. If applicable, and it often is, I chime in with, "Your librarian is the perfect person for something like this!"

Having not been trained as school librarians, many administrators are unaware of the school librarian's magic! Speak up and get involved!

Finding just the right hashtag for yourself or your teachers has gotten easier over time. Jerry Blumengarten (@Cybraryman1) was the first (that I am aware of) to begin compiling a list of educational hashtag Twitter chats as they emerged. Other companies like Nurph (now defunct) and Participate Learn have also moved into the Twitter chat organization realm, making efforts to locate a hashtag that matches your education specialty, participating in chats, and archiving past chats an easy, stress-free process.

CHAPTER 7

Video and Social Media

The combination of video and social media has created overnight stars out of ordinary people. Students can learn on their own through videos shared via social media, and they can also create their own videos to showcase their individual talents and expertise. School librarians can help students learn how best to harness these resources.

Video Resources

Unlike the Buggles' song, "Video Killed the Radio Star" implies, video can and is changing the landscape of education in a myriad of ways for both students and educators. Video holds the power for educators to impact student learning 24/7, and make learning *rewindable*, so that all students can learn at their own pace. Video empowers students to be masters of their own learning, and to find and harness the power of their own voice.

YouTube

Youtube dominates the video/television market among young people within our student demographic. My six-year-old grandson is so enthralled with shows on YouTube that his mother put him on YouTube restriction and now limits his viewing time. One of the biggest draws on YouTube for children, and the one that prompted restriction for my grandson, is videos of people providing live narration while playing video games. Even my high school students are affixed to their phones, watching these videos. In fact, "Gaming videos got so popular, YouTube split them off into their own section called YouTube Gaming" (commonsensemedia.org/website-reviews/youtube-gaming).

Schools that block student access to YouTube are severely crippling student learning, and are failing to teach students how to master their own learning.

Khan Academy

Khan Academy began simply; Salman Khan started helping his cousin with difficult math problems via video. Word got out about the "free tutoring sessions" Khan was providing and as word spread, demand for his tutoring videos increased. He turned to YouTube as a repository for his tutoring videos, and Khan Academy was born.

Khan Academy serves up instructional videos, excercises, and a personalized learning dashboard to allow students to learn at their own pace. According to the webiste, "Khan Academy tackles "math, science, computer programming, history, art history, economics, and more. Our math missions guide learners from kindergarten to calculus using state-of-the-art, adaptive technology that identifies strengths and learning gaps" (KhanAcademy.com, n.d.).

Flipped Classroom

Educators like Aaron Sams (@chemicalsams) and Jon Bergmann (@jonbergmann) led the way in using video in the classroom by creating what they coined a "flipped classroom." The simplest definition of a flipped classroom is "a pedagogical model in which the typical lecture and homework elements of a course are reversed. Short video lectures are viewed by students at home before the class session, while in-class time is devoted to exercises, projects, or discussions" (Educause, 2012).

Unfortunately, many educators have oversimplified the intent and nature of the flipped classroom and have become disillusioned with the idea. Instead of looking at a video as a way to flip the classroom, I choose to see video as a way to "make learning rewindable," as Kevin Honeycutt (@kevinhoneycutt) says. I can't tell you how many math classes I sat through, feeling hopelessly lost and completely stupid because I missed parts of the lesson or needed to see certain steps repeated. Of course, I was too embarrassed to ask for help. What I know now is that I wasn't stupid; I just learned in a different way. The same is true of our students. There aren't any stupid students, only students who learn differently. While some students may understand a lesson the first or second time a concept is introduced, it might take other students ten, twenty, fifty, or more times watching the lesson, rewinding, fast-forwarding, and practicing before they grasp the same concept. In the end, all students feel successful and the concept has been mastered.

Live Interactive Video Tools

Instead of having students or student groups present at the front of the class, allow them to broadcast and record their presentations using live, interactice video. Now their presentation has a real-world audience with real-world feedback. Using live video in this manner allows students to see good and bad digital citizenship in action and may make them think twice about what they say, do, and post online in the future.

Periscope

Periscope is a live video app that allows people to broadcast what is happening around them in real time through their Twitter feed. Viewers of Periscope videos can comment and add reactions in real time as the video is being broadcast.

Educator and blogger at Tomorrow's Learners, Sam Gibson offers the following ideas for using Periscope in the classroom:

- Show real-world evidence for inquiry projects.

- Stream presentations/speeches that students make.

- Gain feedback and information from a wider audience. (Gibson, 2015)

But the possibilities don't end there. Gibson also suggests ways Periscope can be used outside of the classroom—including live streams of school trips and sporting or cultural events—and by teachers for professional development.

Facebook Live

Facebook Live is the newest addition to the live interactive video-streaming phenomenon. Similar to Periscope, Facebook Live allows users to broadcast live video feeds through their Facebook stream, and for viewers to comment or react in real time. Like most social media, Facebook Live has come under scrutiny as people have used it in sometimes shockingly horrific ways. It is our job as educators to teach and model proper use of Facebook Live and other social media tools.

YouTube Live

My favorite video-recording tool by far is YouTube Live (formerly Google Hangouts on Air). YouTube Live is simple, quick, and easy to set up: all you need is a computer with a camera and microphone. Even better, there is no need to download or convert the video when you are finished broadcasting because YouTube Live automatically places your video on your YouTube channel for you. YouTube provides various privacy and sharing options for your recordings to fit most needs. A closed captioning feature can be used to accommodate the needs of hearing-impaired students.

Lee's Summit R–7 school district in Lee's Summit, Missouri, has an all-inclusive Google Hangouts guide for teachers. While most of the resources have not been updated since the switch to YouTube Live, the collaborative Google Document (sites.google. com/site/gpluseduhangouts/ideas) contains a collaborative list of creative ideas collected from the #eduhangout group. You can even submit your own ideas, detailing how you have used Google Hangouts to connect your classroom.

Online Tutoring

Billy Ramsey, high school mathematics teacher and football coach at Auburn High School in Auburn, Alabama, started using video tutorials with his students as a way to provide tutoring for his football players who couldn't stay after school for traditional tutoring sessions. Mr. Ramsey first started using the recording feature on his SMART Board; he embedded the videos on his learning management page for students to access at anytime. During a Tech Tips Library session Mr. Ramsey was turned on to Google Hangouts on Air (now YouTube Live). Eager to try new resources to enhance student learning, Mr. Ramsey began offering live tutoring sessions to his students one evening per week. Mr. Ramsey app smashed Twitter and his Google Hangout sessions with a special hashtag for students to use to ask questions during the live tutoring sessions. (App smashing is when you use multiple apps to create projects.) The best thing about these tutoring sessions is that the tutoring sessions, when using Google Hangouts on Air, are automatically recorded and available for viewing on YouTube. This way, students who participated in the live sessions could review the video as they worked through assignments. Additionally, students who were unable to attend the live sessions have access to the recording and can use it, as well as the hashtag, to gain a better understanding of new mathematical concepts.

Virtual Debates

My friend Elissa Malespina (@elissamalespina), introduced me to the possibilities of holding student conferences and debates via Google Hangouts on Air as a way to connect students without the cost of travel, hotels, and food. Here is how this worked: Elissa's eighth-grade debate team students needed to debate another eighth-grade team, but there wasn't money in the budget for the expenses normally associated with attending conferences or other connections between schools and districts. Elissa found another eighth-grade school that was willing to connect via a virtual debate. The next step was to secure judges, and ensure that these judges could be at both school locations at the same time. Enter Google Hangouts on Air, where up to ten people can see one another and converse in real time—from anywhere! Ta da! Using social media and her PLN, Elissa requested judges via Twitter. I jumped at the chance and secured a spot for my high school debate team students to judge the debates. Other judges included Elissa's superintendent, other teachers and administrators from around the country, and a teacher (my favorite "judge") who signed up his whole fourth-grade class to listen to and evaluate the debates using a rubric provided by Elissa.

Read Across America Day

During that same school year, I used YouTube Live to connect my Spanish 1 and 2 teacher with a class in Mexico City for Read Across America Day. Both classes had read the books, *To Kill a Mockingbird* and *Go Set a Watchman* by Harper Lee. I was floored by the depth of the conversation as these students compared and contrasted the characters from both books, explored issues of racism, and even discussed the upcoming U.S. election. Students undoubtedly gained a much deeper understanding of the novels because they were exposed to ideas beyond the four walls of their respective classrooms.

Skype

Skype in the Classroom is another much loved video connection tool used by many teachers around the world. Perhaps one of the most known Skype activities used by teachers is Mystery Skype, a "global guessing game that gets kids learning about geography, culture, and the similarities and differences of how children live all over the world" (Microsoft, 2017). The Mystery Skype website, in conjunction with Twitter and the hashtag #MysterySkype, can get both you and your class connected and learning in just a short amount of time, and it is a learning experience your students will cherish. I know many teachers who have set goals to play Mystery Skype with at least one class from each state. How fun! In addition to participating in Mystery Skype experiences, teachers can use Skype to:

- Skype with an author;

- connect with other classrooms;

- connect with experts;

- offer tutoring;

- host a virtual career exploration day;

- practice a foreign language;

- practice interviews; and

- host parent teacher conferences.

The Educational Technology and Mobile Learning blog has a very detailed post entitled, The Complete Guide to the Use of Skype in Education (educatorstechnology.com/2012/06/complete-guide-to-use-of-skype-in.html). Examples from the site include using Skype to help langauge learning by connecting with a native speaker, and students completing history project by collaborating with the curator of a natural history museum.

Live Interactive Video Ideas

Modeling use of live interactive social media tools can assist schools in their efforts to disseminate information to students that they will actually watch. Some ideas for how to model use of video tools such as Periscope and Facebook Live in school include:

- broadcast important addresses from the superintendent, principal, athletic director, or coach;

- spotlight teachers, parents, students, alumni, or board members;

- offer glimpses into cool school classroom projects;

- arrange a virtual visit to a cultural institution or landmark;

- feature departments, programs, and extracurriculars;

- create a student "update" news broadcast;

- connect classes with eachother or with content-area experts, and interact with students;

- stream live news events for your students;

- broadcast a weekly wrap-up for your classes;

- conduct virtual office hours for your students;

- reach absent students;

- conduct athlete signings;

- host live Q&A tutorials and exam reviews; and

- broadcast bad weather reports.

Instagram and SnapChat Video Tools

While not interactive in real time, Instagram and Snapchat allow users to create short videos that can then be shared with followers. Instagram allows up to sixty seconds of video recording. Snapchat allows ten-second videos.

Innovative teachers know that using these tools introduces a whole new twist on learning in their classrooms. Using these tools captures your students' attention (this is "their space"), and it gives you opportunities to model professional use. Some ideas for using video features in Instagram and Snapchat include:

- introduce new content in a fun, new way;

- use video as a formative assessment to check for student understanding;

- let students create a ten-second video to demonstrate understanding of a topic;

- provide meaningful, personal feedback to students with regards to their progress on projects or other classroom tasks;

- record class reminders about homework, tests, and upcoming school events;

- record classroom activities to share with parents and colleagues;

- post questions that tie back to your lesson or goal of the day; and

- have students create book talk videos.

Blocking of Video Sites and Apps

When teacher groups discuss the numerous benefits of video in the classroom, their cheif complaint is access. Their ability to access YouTube Live or other video apps is either blocked by their district-level technology department or disallowed by their administrators (and sometimes both!). Most administrators say these tools are blocked for student safety, we need to redefine our definition of "safety." Are we really keeping students safe when we ban tools instead of teaching proper use within the controlled environment of our schools, where we can lessen the high-stakes consequences of failure?

Naturally, students are going to make mistakes while using devices at school or elsewhere. One of the most common mistakes students make is using the video feature of their device or video apps inappropriately; this is a *good* thing. When students inevitably post video of other people to social media without permission, it presents the administration with the perfect opportunity to teach respect, the right to privacy, and good digital citizenship skills. We can't take advantage of teach-able moments if students aren't granted access to social media platforms in the first place. It's so much better for students to make their mistakes with devices and social media in a safe environment specifically because it allows educators to correct mistakes and prepare students for college and career.

I once worked in a BYOD school where the administrator became enraged at a less than flattering video of him a student had posted without his permission. His reaction was not to teach but to punish, and not just the student who posted the video, but the entire school. He banned cell phones for the rest of the school year, in a BYOD school! Students could still bring tablets and laptops, just no cell phones. The only thing this actually accomplished was alienating the majority of both students and teachers.

Perhaps a better reaction would have been one that turned the incident into a learning experience. Why not require students who used video inappropriately to research, design, and create a green screen space for the school? These students could use the space to create a public service announcement (PSA) about responsible use of video features and apps on their devices. Students could take it a step further and create how-to tutorials for using the green screen space with a variety of devices, and the rest of the school could use the space for academic endeavors.

By eliminating the chance to turn instances of misuse into teachable moments, we are putting our students at grave risk. MTV aired a series in 2010, "Sexting in America: When Privates Go Public," outlining the types of trouble students can get themselves into while using video apps, including convicted students who must register as sex offenders for the rest of their lives (MTV, 2017). The devastating, life altering, permanent stigmas that students face when social media is misused are exactly the reasons why we should teach rather than ban video apps.

CHAPTER 8

Books and Social Media

Reading is no longer a solitary act. Ebooks allow readers to easily share passages and favorite quotes to their social media feeds. Some social media sites allow readers to rate and review books. Others allow readers to create their own fan fiction (stories that continue where the original story ends). Additionally, budding authors are bypassing the traditional route with publishing companies by self-publishing books and promoting them through social media.

Kids are social. They crave interaction with others about all of their activities, including what they are reading. Even the most introverted students want to find others who like to read similar content. Social media can give all students a voice and help them find "their people."

Book Clubs

If you have ever tried to start a book club at your school, you may have run into some of the difficulties I've encountered. Students want to be part of the club but are unable to meet before or after school due to transportation or other issues. Other students may already have other club obligations that conflict with the book club's scheduled events. Once students attend club meetings, they may find that their genres of choice vary widely, and agreeing on a book everyone in the club will read is a challenge. Or, even worse, only a very small handful have the time or interest to be part of a school book club.

GoodReads

Perhaps one of the most popular social media sites for books is Goodreads. Social media sites like Goodreads bring people together through their taste in books. In particular, Goodreads provides more than a few great tools that school librarians can use to their advantage.

At one school, to combat some of these issues with getting a book club started, I decided to go entirely digital with the library-sponsored school book club. I named it Not Your Average Book Club. Because we were a Google School, I set up a Google Classroom for students who wanted to join. Once students signed up to the Google Classroom they were directed to join our Goodreads group and to use the Goodreads reading challenge to set a reading goal for themselves. Students were encouraged to use our Google Classroom page and the Goodreads group to share what they were reading, recommend books they had already read, and share books they thought they might read next. Through our Google Classroom, I also gave students the task of spending over half of our book supply funding by recommending books we should add to our school library collection.

The Somewhat Virtual Book Club

I wanted students to comprehend the power of social media and experience the ability to connect with people from around the world, including authors. I encouraged my students to participate in the Somewhat Virtual Book Club. As of this writing, the club is composed of fifteen high schools across the United States plus one Japanese high school. The book club allows each member school to choose one of the monthly book selections and create applicable points of discussion. Students from all fifteen schools meet virtually, using YouTube Live, the first Wednesday of each month, and they discuss the selected book. We also invite the book's author to join the conversation. Elizabeth Wein, author of *Code Name Verity*, joined one of these meetings from her home in Scotland, and spent over an hour talking with our students!

The Somewhat Virtual Book Club focuses on books appropriate for high school readers. If you are a librarian at a middle or elementary school, you might want to use the Book Club for Kids podcast (bookclubforkids.org) to connect your students. There are a variety of ways your students can participate, from simply listening to the postcast to submitting book recommendations or questions for their favorite authors to answer.

Alternatives to Book Clubs

Still can't seem to find the right fit for you and your students, but want your students to be connected? Have your students find their favorite author on Twitter and tweet them a question or comment about their book(s). Start your own podcast or vodcast book-sharing series, and invite other schools through your PLN. Jake Duncan, a bilingual immersion educator and founder of The Campfire (www.thecampfi.re), set up great examples of a vodcast and how to provide a place where students can have a voice. I am dying to replicate Duncan's idea at my school library. It's something that can easily be adjusted to fit any school and any age group.

Fan Fiction

My students have expressed interest in creating fan fiction (also sometimes known as "fanfic"). While there are several differing explanations of fan fiction, journalist Lev Grossman best described the phenomenon as:

> "[W]hat literature might look like if it were reinvented from scratch after a nuclear apocalypse by a band of brilliant pop-culture junkies trapped in a sealed bunker . . . The writers write it and put it up online just for the satisfaction. They're fans, but they're not silent, couch-bound consumers of media. The culture talks to them, and they talk back to the culture in its own language" (Grossman, 2011).

Some of you might be thinking at this point, "Oh no! What about copyright?" This has been a bone of contention between the fan fiction world and authors. Some authors welcome fan fiction and even post links to the most popular fan fiction works on their own websites. Others are completely against any form of fan fiction and actively send cease and desist letters to creators of fan fiction based on their books. Then there are authors like Orson Scott Card (best known for the *Enders Game* series), who once posted on his author website: "to write fiction using my characters is morally identical to moving into my house without invitation and throwing out my family," but completely changed his mind and has since has supported fan fiction contests. He even defended his support in the Wall Street Journal: "Every piece of fan fiction is an ad for my book. What kind of idiot would I be to want that to disappear?" (Alter, 2012).

For me, I see fan fiction as a great way to get students reading and writing. I always encourage my students to write, be it fan fiction or other outlets, and will try to follow their writing, if possible, and comment on their progress and what I liked about what they wrote.

If you are looking to get your students involved in writing fan fiction, there are several sites that promote or sponsor it. A word of caution first: please be careful about what sites you recommend to students. Some of these sites contain access to adult-themed writings (think *Fifty Shades of Gray*). Here are a few sites to get started. A post on the Ebook Friendly blog titled "15 most popular fanfiction websites" contains a comprehensive list (ebookfriendly.com/fan-fiction-websites/)

- **FanFiction** (fanfiction.net) is the largest fanfiction archive, with over 2 million users actively reading, sharing, following, and reviewing fan fiction.

- **Quotev** (quotev.com/fanfic) features more than 15 categories of fanfiction where users can share stories and interact via quizzes, polls, and surveys.

- **Kindle Worlds** (kindleworlds.amazon.com) is Amazon's fan fiction platform, offering fan fiction ebooks for sale (sample chapters are free but most books cost

$0.99–$3.00) as well as a publishing platform for fan fiction authors. (Kowalczyk, 2017).

Story Wars

One fan fiction site that works a little bit differently than the others previously listed is Story Wars (storywars.net). Story Wars is a collaborative fan fiction site that caters more toward schools. Here's how it works, according to the website:

- You can either create your own story or continue on someone else's.

- After two drafts have been added for a chapter, a countdown starts. This is the remaining time when other people can add new drafts for the chapter.

- When the countdown has reached zero, a voting round will start, featuring all the drafts that [were] added.

- The draft receiving the most votes is added to the growing story. Then the process begins all over again. (StoryWars.net, n.d.)

One possible way to get your students using Story Wars is to have them actively participate in the reading and voting process; encourage them to enter their own chapters to be voted on as well.

To have more control over the process, Story Wars also offers a classroom version of their service (storywars.net/classroom). This service allows you to begin a story that can be seen by only your students, and accessed through a unique link. This service also provides an analytics tool so you can easily follow each student's writing progress, check for readability level of their writing, and use other teacher-friendly features.

The Power of (Self-)Publishing

Writing fan fiction may inspire some students to write their own, original stories. I love it when my students create worlds and characters of their own. so I encourage them to keep writing. Due to the rise of the internet, people no longer need to navigate the complicated book publishing industry. More and more budding authors are going the route of self-publishing, which allows them to publish books as physical print copies, ebooks, or both.

When my children were in first grade, they wrote and illustrated their own books. Their teacher, Ms. Elder, bound the books and sent them home with each child. I still cherish these books, and now my grandchildren are reading the books their parents wrote in the first grade. The warmth in my heart radiates just thinking about it. Schools are beginning to realize that their own students and teachers can write books and ebooks that can be added to the school collection for distribution.

Michele Nokleby, school librarian at Hawthorne elementary in Missoula, Montana, presented a TEDxMCPS Teachers Talk in 2012 about publishing student work online. (You can watch it at youtu.be/A-eRv7DRoiA.) The idea to publish student work in various ebook formats came about naturally through her school's lunchtime writing club. Instead of sending these books home (like the precious books my children had created in the first grade), Michele added them to the shelves of the library to be checked out. She wanted the ability to share these great books with a larger audience, and concluded that the digitization of the books was the next step in publishing and sharing. Michele chose ebook sites that offered readers the option to download the book in electronic format or purchase a hardcover print copy. Thus, the parents or grandparents could always have a special memento to cherish.

Michele, like most superstar librarians, was not satisfied with merely providing an ebook. She also wanted to capture the emotive quality of students' voices, and she found a site where students could record themselves reading their books. This way, younger students who were not independent readers could also enjoy the ebook experience. Michele incorporated podcast opportunities to showcase student poetry, and she created blogging opportunities for children at her school. She used the blog posts as a way to teach good digital citizenship through the use of the comments sections, making sure students knew how to leave "responsible, respectful, and productive" comments (Nokleby, 2012).

Michele's favorite project was revamping the traditionally dry book reports and kicking them up a notch through student-created book trailers. Creating book trailers amped up learning—book reports became more than just summaries, and they required important digital age skills for using computers, video, images, music, and understanding copyright.

When I asked Michele about the TED talk, she said one of the driving motivators was to showcase just how critical a library with a certified librarian is to a school. The newly hired superintendent for her district had replaced all school librarians with clerks in his last school district, a tragedy she did not want to see happen to the students and teachers at the school she loved so dearly.

Buffy Hamilton (also known as The Unquiet Librarian), has always been on top of the newest technologies, especially those applicable to school libraries, and she has fearlessly and boldly led the way into uncharted territory, sharing her stories of successes and failures with the rest of us. In 2016, Buffy blazed a trail into the ebook world through a collaborative project with Ms. Amy Balogh's English for Speakers of Other Languages (ESOL) class in Georgia: *Twelve Worlds, One Book* was published.

"This book is an anthology of student writing created by Ms. Balogh's [ESOL] students crafted as part of the work they crafted in Ms. Balogh's writer's workshop approach to composition instruction. The book contains many pieces of writing, including poetry, short stories, essays, memoirs, monologues, plays, a biosketch, and microfiction." (Hamilton, 2017)

This experience has left a lasting positive effect on the students (and their teacher), and Buffy is hopeful more teachers will be encouraged to create ebooks of their own.

Even *The New York Times* has recognized this phenomenon and now features a bestseller list for ebooks, which is compiled based on sales reported from Amazon, Barnes and Noble, Apple, and Google. One of the most successful ebooks to achieve *New York Times* bestseller status is *The Martian* by Andy Weir. *The Martian* got its humble beginnings as an online serial novel; it sold 35,000 ebook copies on Amazon before being picked up by Crown Publishing Group.

Self-published Amazon author Ronnie Sidney, II, MSW, is one of the most heartwarming examples of using the power of social media to gain an audience. His first book, *Nelson Beats the Odds*, was an Amazon bestseller in the Kindle store learning disability category. Ronnie states, "The most common piece of advice I've heard from successful authors is to start a blog" (Sidney, 2016).

The blog's success helped Ronnie secure interviews and speaking engagements, and increased book sales, but much of this success was also due to Ronnie's self-promotion through social media. He promoted his book on Facebook, Twitter, Instagram, Tumblr, and Snapchat and joined several Facebook groups with large followings. In school, Ronnie was identified as learning disabled, and placed in special education classes. Despite the odds against him, started his own business and subsequently published three novels (and counting).

How many students in our schools are just like Ronnie? As school librarians, we are in a unique position to find each child's unique talents and present them with opportunities and examples through which they can shine.

CHAPTER 9

Social Media Managers

What school librarian has time to post to multiple sites, or for that matter, read posts from multiple sites? How can we be expected to keep up with the latest trends and make sense of the information saturating our plethora of ever-growing social media feeds? This chapter examines social media tools that can help librarians keep up with the latest trends without monopolizing their time. These tools can streamline your social media into something manageable, helpful, and hopefully stress-reducing.

Twitter Chats

Twitter chats are one of the best free, twenty-four hour professional development "conferences" you can attend, and you can do it while in your pajamas, eating ice cream! There are Twitter chats available for practically any education area you can imagine. If there isn't one for your specialty area, all you have to do is start one and spread the word!

I often liken Twitter chats to the "I Love Lucy" episode where Lucy and Ethel are working on the assembly line wrapping chocolates. I envision that each chocolate coming down the assembly line is a tweet in the Twitter chat stream of conversation. The chat starts out slow with introductions; who you are, where you are from, and what subjects or grades you teach. You think to yourself, just like Ethel and Lucy did, "This isn't so bad. I can handle this!" Then the real conversation gets started: leading questions are posed by the Twitter chat moderator(s). Now the tweets (chocolates) are rolling down the Twitter stream (assembly line) at a pace too quick for all of the tweets to be read (wrapped). On top of this, you might be receiving direct messages and notifications. That's at least three different streams with tweets that you want to read. How can you make any sense of the hour-long Twitter chat when you are frantically clicking between the Twitter chat stream, your direct message stream, and your notifications stream?

Luckily, many others encountered this same dilemma, so Twitter chat aides were created. The most popular Twitter chat aides among the educators I know include HootSuite, TweetDeck, and Participate Learning Chats. You might be thinking, "What's wrong with just using Twitter for a Twitter chat?" That is perfectly logical thinking, but with the speed of chats and the various streams to keep track of during the conversation, these aides will remove a great deal of the stress associated with such a quick and vibrant conversation.

I'VE USED HOOTSUITE, EVERYPOST, AND TWEETDECK

Ashley Cooksey

I love Tweetdeck for our monthly chats because I can schedule the posts & set columns so that I can watch our chat and my notifications at the same time.

Figure 9.1 Ashley Cooksey's Tweetdeck testimonial.

When I first started using a Twitter chat aide, I tried out both HootSuite and TweetDeck. Both of these Twitter chat aides organize your tweets into hashtag streams. All of your streams are lined up in columns next to one another. Your Twitter chat stream, your notifications, and your direct messaging streams become much more manageable. Personally, I found HootSuite was a bit slower and didn't have as many distractions for a first-time user. Gradually, as I became more accustomed to the ebb and flow of most Twitter chats, I found that TweetDeck was better suited to my personal needs. The best way to know which one will work best for you is to take them both for a test drive.

If you have never participated in a Twitter chat session before, don't do it alone! Get some of your teacher and librarian friends together and make a fun night out of it. I learned this brilliant idea from my former assistant principals, Jennifer Hogan and Holly Sutherland. These two inspiring leaders not only started and moderate the #ALEdChat sessions each Monday night at 8 P.M. PT/10 P.M. ET, they also started (and help moderate) the #USEdChat sessions that bring individual state Twitter chats together for one night each quarter (see Figure 9.2). To assist teachers with learning the ins-and-outs of Twitter chats—how to tweet, how to respond to a tweet, what is a hashtag, what is a direct message, where are my direct messages, and similar questions—Jennifer and Holly arranged for teachers to meet at a Twitter party during a #USEdChat session in our school library.

Figure 9.2 #USEdchat.

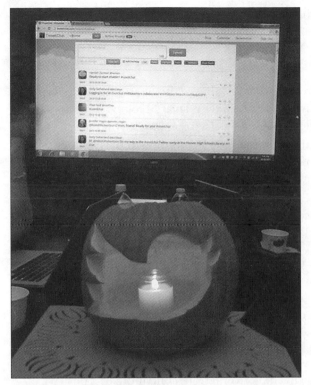

Figure 9.3 #USEdChat session Twitter party.

Not only were teachers lured with yummy treats and the ability to wear pajamas to school at night, but we also knew that we were in a safe learning environment together. We knew no one would think less of us if we were completely lost. To hear teachers literally squeal in delight when someone responded to their comment during the chat was electrifying. Just imagine that type of response from your students! Near the end of the hour (most Twitter chats are an hour long), a teacher who was participating in a Twitter chat for the first time said, "What? The chat is almost over? We just got started!"

Time flies during a Twitter chat session. Here are a few things to keep in mind.

Don't try to read every tweet. Good tweets will be retweeted.

Don't open links that are shared during the Twitter chat itself. Many educators share relevant blog posts or articles related to the topic of the Twitter chat. If you take the time to go out and view the blog post, you will have missed a good chunk of the conversation by the time you get back to the chat. A good Twitter chat will have moderators who archive the chat, so that you can go back and peruse the shared resources at a later time, and at a more leisurely pace.

Do engage in side conversations. Sometimes people will respond to something you tweeted during the chat. Maybe they want to ask a question or discuss it in further detail. These side conversations are great opportunities for connecting and building your PLN.

Do find new people to add to your PLN. Watch for people who engage in the conversation, contribute in a positive manner, and provide great resource links. These are key people to continue learning from as part of your PLN.

Do block anyone who is abusive. Twitter chats are open to the entire world, so anyone can jump into the conversation. If someone is being abusive, do not engage them in conversation. Just block and report them. It's not worth your time to try and combat an internet troll.

Do view Gwyneth Jones' Tweet Like a Ninja slideshare. You, too can Tweet like a ninja following Gwyneth's six easy steps. Google it; you won't be disappointed!

Organizing Resources

I am a resource hoarder. I follow a staggering number of interesting educators and others on Twitter. I belong to a multitude of Facebook groups. I like to keep up with blog posts and websites that cover a variety of topics in which I am interested. Simply visiting each site, each person, and each resource would be more than a full-time job. To assist with taming the flow of information, I use a tool that feeds all of these resources into one convenient location. Some websites and apps that can assist with this seemingly overwhelming task include: Paper.li, Scoop.it, Instapaper, FlipBoard, and Pocket.

Figure 9.4 Paper.li information feed.

Paper.li

According to its website, Paper.li is "a content curation service that lets you turn socially shared content into beautiful online newspapers and newsletters." I love the newspaper layout because it makes zeroing in on the content I want to read as easy as scanning the headlines in a print newspaper, but without the black ink left behind on your fingers.

Paper.li pulls information from the web based on the search parameters you set up in your account. Paper.li can search the web by keywords, search Twitter by hashtags, gather posts by RSS feed, and can even add information shared via Facebook groups and pages. You can add information from your favorite YouTube channels, or combine information curated on Scoop.it, Pinterest, and Instagram.

You can also build customized Paper.lis that will curate information for particular purposes or topics and set up automatic share settings to share your customized Paper.li with your PLN. There is even an option to create a collaborative Paper.li with your students, teachers, school, district, or other professional or personal communities.

Scoop.it

Scoop.it is "part content curation tool, part social network," allowing you to "create boards of curated content based on topics you choose, share your thoughts on that content, and connect with others who have similar interests" (Scoop.it.com). Basically, Scoop.it scours the internet based on the search terms you designate and retrieves information in the form of "scoops." You can also add your own "scoops" while surfing the web, interacting on social media sites, and so on, with the Scoop.it bookmarklet feature. The difference with Scoop.it is in its social component; you can have conversations about various scoops gathered in your topic-specific scoop sections.

I tried Scoop.it because my library hero, Gwyneth Jones, loves it and uses it all the time. In fact, Gwyneth loves Scoop.it so much, she has a pro account and is a rewards member! (Side note: I use to think Gwyneth was saying "Stup-it," but she was really saying "Scoop.it." I was so confused!) You can take a look at how Gwyneth is utilizing Scoop.it here: scoop.it/u/gwynethjones.

Instapaper and Pocket

Instapaper and Pocket are both tools used to save content so it can be read later on a different device, such as an e-reader, smartphone, or tablet. I tried Instapaper when it first came out and found that the visual layout didn't suit my taste. I soon moved over to Pocket, which has a more Pinterest-like visual appeal. Whichever you decide to use is really up to your personal preferences.

Confession: I also only really use Pocket when I can't get a blog post or article I am reading to save to one of my Pinterest boards. I'm a self-admitted Pinterest addict!

Feedly

Feedly is another aggregator that compiles news feeds from a variety of online sources into a convenient format for reading and sharing with others. Within Feedly, school librarians and other educators can create topic-specific boards to share information gathered from keywords and specific URLs (like your favorite blogs). You can easily share gathered resources to various social media sites like Twitter, Facebook, Pocket, OneNote, Instapaper, and more. Based on how you program the initial settings, Feedly offers suggestions of other content that complements your topics of interest. Feedly also has a "read later" feature that comes in handy on those super busy days.

Flipboard

Think of Flipboard as a personalized magazine that you can take anywhere. Based on your interest and keywords, the app gathers stories from around the web and "delivers them to you in an attractive visual feed" (Angove, 2013). I like it because it has a slick magazine feel to it, which appeals to my need for visual stimulation. I also like Flipboard because you can easily share information you read on Flipboard to various social media sites. My evening relaxation before bedtime is to read through Flipboard stories and save the articles that catch my attention to a corresponding Pinterest topic board.

If you like the look and feel of Flipboard, you might also think about using customized Flipboard magazines with your students. Below are a few examples of how teachers are utilizing Flipboard in their classrooms/schools:

- Michael Brody uses Flipboard as a syllabus and course content planner. His customized FlipBoard, Things AP Econ Students Should Know, can be viewed at flipboard.com/@brodymichael/things-ap-econ-students-should-know-bpio7up9z.

- Kimberley S. Cox uses Flipboard for class projects. Students are tasked with compiling editorials, images and YouTube videos around specific subject matter they're studying in your class. They can do this individually, or in groups.

- Jacqueline Mezquita uses Flipboard as an educational resource guide.

- Sue Waters uses Flipboard as a collaborative tool where students and teacher groups can "compile articles, teaching resources or how-to videos related to the subject you teach or education in general and share that magazine with other educators in your school or district."

- Zach Morrow uses Flipboard to keep parents informed by creating a magazine with curriculum examples, class readings, suggested at home projects, images from class and classroom updates flipped in from a personal blog.

- As an administrator, Callie Walker uses Flipboard as a "way for [her] school to stay in touch with students, parents and the community. As long as your school paper, newsletter or event images are available as an RSS feed or via social media, you can search for it on Flipboard. You can also use web tools to flip your school's posts into new magazines—into which you can even mix in other content—around any topic you like."

Pinterest

Pinterest is a social network that allows users to visually share and discover new interests by posting (known as "pinning") images or videos to boards (i.e., a collection of "pins," with a common theme) and browsing what other users have pinned. Pinterest is where I store valuable internet information that I want to easily access later. I have two separate Pinterest accounts: one personal. and one professional. My professional account contains boards for every subject area in the school plus much, much more.

I especially like the Pinterest board I curate for the school as a whole. Other teacher collaborators and I can add resources that normally clog up school email to the school's shared Pinterest board. This has the added benefit of convenience: the resources can easily be located without the aggravation of sifting through a lifetime of emails, trying to remember who sent what resource when.

Posting to Multiple Sites

IFTTT

IFTTT stands for If This, Then That. IFTTT lets users create recipes or applets where some type of event in one device or service automatically triggers an action in another. For example, I have one IFTTT recipe or applet that will automatically tweet anything I add to Pinterest when I include the hashtag #TLChat in the description of the pin.

Creating new recipes or applets can be a bit confusing at first, so try some of the pre-made applets under the "Discover" section on IFTTT. Once you have created your recipes, your social media posting will be so much easier.

Buffer

Buffer is known as your personal social media assistant. Buffer allows you to create as many Tweets, Facebook stories, or LinkedIn updates as you want, and Buffer posts them for you throughout the day at times designed to reach your desired audience. You can also override the automated posting feature and specify dates and times you want Buffer to post.

Buffer is great for those of us who can't post to social media throughout the day. Mostly I post to social media at night as I wind down from a busy day, which floods my social media feeds with a burst of information all at once. With Buffer my posts go out over time, so I don't drown my followers with an influx of information.

If you are using social media to help promote the exciting things going on in your library (events, new books, makerspace fun, etc.), Buffer is a great way to schedule those posts!

I USE BUFFER WITH INSTAGRAM AND FACEBOOK

Debbie Jones

I like Buffer because I can spend an hour setting up my posts for the next three days and then not have to worry about it unless I want to add more posts.

Figure 9.5 Debbie Jones on using Buffer.

Instagram

Instagram is one of the top social media platforms for reaching secondary education students. It has a great feature that sends your Instagram post to multiple sites (like Facebook, Twitter, Tumblr, Flickr, and Swarm) at one time. You select the posts and social media outlets in which you want each post to appear.

You Must Never Sleep

I have PLN friends who often comment, "You must never sleep!" Believe me, I love my sleep! I use some of these social media managers to work smarter, not harder. I love that because I utilize these tools I am better able to keep up with the latest news, trends, and events that relate to topics that matter in my daily life. I encourage you to try out some of the social media managers mentioned here, and see what suits your personal style and needs. When you do, you will be amazed at how your knowledge base will grow exponentially without requiring more of an investment of your limited time.

PART THREE

Stay Connected

CHAPTER 10

Connected Librarians

Social media is one of the best, most useful, and free professional development tools available. In this chapter, we will explore ways that school librarians can use social media to build their own PLNs.

Let's face it: life as a school librarian is professionally isolating. Sure, we have our wonderful students who make our days full of adventure (you never know what kids will do or say), but we lack a peer group that "gets us." In most schools, especially in this day and age of severe budget cuts, a librarian is often the only person in our school who understands his or her role in the overall school structure. We don't really fit in the administrative peer group, nor do we fit comfortably in the teacher peer group. We are, as they say, an island unto ourselves.

If you are lucky and work in a larger school, you might earn enough student credits for an library aide, two certified school librarians, or both. In the best scenario, you at least have a peer group of three people. In a common scenario, you are the only person in your school who knows what you do. Worst-case scenario, you're the only secondary education librarian in your district.

Isolated Much?

The size of your school district and whether it sets aside distr-tic-wide professional development time for school librarians to meet also determines the level to which one is isolated. Sadly, many school districts do not allow this important time for their school librarians. Instead, librarians attend regular teacher professional development sessions that rarely have anything to do with the unique concerns of school libraries. In most of the school districts where I have worked, I have either been the only high school librarian or just one of two. So, even within a school district that sets aside professional development time for district librarians to meet, secondary education librarians often remain isolated because the conversations focus mainly on elementary schools.

Finding Your People

A peer group is important because it connects you to someone who can share or listen to ideas, help you stay motivated, and even offer a shoulder to cry on from time to time. When I found Shelly Terrell and her 30 Goals Teacher ReBoot Camp and, subsequently, the #EdChat Twitter chat sessions, it was the first time in my career that I felt like I was really connecting and learning with other educators. Their ideas were fresh, fun, bold, innovative, and exciting! They were different from anything I had heard in my school district. Yet, I wasn't completely satisfied with my conversations through the #EdChat hashtag. I wanted something more focused on my specialized role within the educational setting.

#TLChat

Bitten by the Twitter chat bug, it wasn't long before I approached the Alabama School Library Association (ASLA) with a proposal to start a state library Twitter chat session. I wanted a place for school librarians from across the state to discuss topics relevant to school libraries and librarians. We set up a monthly date and time, created a hashtag, and began spreading the word. Soon, we had librarians from around the country joining in our librarian-centered Twitter chats.

It was around this same time that I discovered the TL Virtual Cafe library group led by Gwyneth Jones, Tiffany Whitehead, and Joyce Valenza (tlvirtualcafe.wikispaces.com). The TL Virtual Cafe provides free, monthly professional development webinars specifically designed for school librarians—something much needed for school librarians nationwide.

I had been promoting the ASLA Twitter chats for nearly a year when Joyce Valenza approached me with an idea to start a national Twitter chat for school librarians.. The ASLA Twitter chats were attended mostly by school librarians from states other than Alabama, it made sense to expand the ASLA Twitter chats to include a national discussion. The #TLChat Twitter chats were merged to be a part of the TL Virtual Cafe.

discussion. The #TLChat Twitter chats were born and merged to be a part of the TL Virtual Cafe.

State Library Twitter Chats

Since the #TLChat Twitter chats were born, there has been a boom of specialized educational hashtags. It wasn't long before state-specific library Twitter chats began appearing on Jerry Blumengarten's educational hashtags page, too. Just this year, Jane Lofton and I worked together to create an easily accessible list of all state-specific school library Twitter chats through a blog crosspost.

 LIBRARY TWITTER CHAT

SCHOOL LIBRARY LIVE TWITTER CHATS ARE CROPPING UP ALL OVER!

by Jane Lofton

School librarians are incredible networkers, and many have discovered that Twitter is one of the very best tools for building and benefiting from a PLN. Those of us taking advantage of Twitter for our PLNs never go a single day without learning about new ideas from our colleagues, and those in related fields. And, Twitter live chats offer a kind of "booster shot" of Twitter goodness in a short amount of time, typically an hour.

A live Twitter chat happens at an announced time. There is always a specific hashtag used to identify the chat. So, you can follow a chat by going to Twitter, searching for the hashtag, selecting Latest, and watching the tweets with that hashtag as people post. You join in by adding that hashtag to each of your own tweets.

Most live Twitter chats take place the same time each month or week. Each session will have a new theme or topic to discuss. Live chats typically have two moderators, who prepare questions in advance and send the questions out during the chat. They start by asking participants to introduce themselves. Then, they use Q1 for question #1, Q2 for question #2, and so on, as a signifier before they post the questions. The questions go out every few minutes. Participants start their responses with A1, A2, and so on. The participants can also interact directly with one another by responding to their posts. At the end, the moderators typically create an archive transcript of the chat so that people who missed the event or want to review it can visit a link and see the conversation.

We can't pretend that live chats are relaxing. They aren't! They are definitely a bit stressful because you see lots of tweets flying by while you are simultaneously trying to think and compose your own answers and comments. At the same time, they are amazingly stimulating, informative, and offer a great chance to interact in real time with your peers and discuss a topic of interest. We have connected with many new Twitter friends and gotten countless wonderful new ideas through chats. Just be prepared in advance that you won't be able to read all the tweets in an active chat; you are bound to miss stuff, and that's O.K. You aren't even obliged to answer all the questions. And, feel free to lurk until you are comfortable.

Educators of all kinds have started live Twitter chats in the last several years, for different subject areas, grade levels, states, regions, and so on. For a list of chats , see Participate's chat site (participate.com/chats) or Cybraryman's Educational Hashtags (cybraryman.com/edhashtags.html). Until recently, though, there was just one live chat specifically for school librarians: #TLChat. The #TLChat hashtag is used by school librarians as one of the main hashtags for targeting school library tweets, but, once a month, it becomes a live chat (on the first Monday of the month at 8:00 p.m. ET). And, joining it as a live chat platform are at least ten state- or regionally-based school library chats. Ever generous as librarians are, we believe that all these chats welcome anyone. For example, you don't have to be from New Jersey to participate in #NJLIBCHAT.

Connected Librarians = Connected Students

Recently, I conducted a survey of school librarians and their experiences using social media in a professional capacity. What follows are their candid responses to my survey questions.

Jane Lofton (@jane_librarian), retired school librarian from Manhattan Beach, California

Throughout the five years I was the teacher librarian at Mira Costa High School (fall 2011–spring 2016), my library club participated in the Somewhat Virtual Book Club (#swvbc), a network of school libraries interested in having live virtual monthly discussions of books. The network was founded by Joyce Valenza, Shannon Miller, and Michelle Luhtala in the fall of 2011, and my school was one of the initial members. This group gave (and continues to give) both small and large groups of students at different schools across the country (and briefly, even internationally) a chance to exchange ideas with students from other schools and regions, and to learn positive meeting and discussion practices. For some of the discussions, the author of the selected book joined us, so students were able to talk to, and ask questions of, the author as well. They also learned about the challenges of connecting with technology when we experienced tech glitches using Google Hangouts, Skype, and Blackboard Collaborate. I was especially proud that, while participants in the group varied from month to month, my school almost never missed a meeting, and four of my students who graduated in 2016 participated for their entire four years at Mira Costa.

Wendy Cope (@wendypcope), Middle School Librarian from Woodstock, Georgia

Putting Star Wars STEM requests out there led to a visit from the 501st—Darth Vader and two storm troopers. It made a good program into a showstopper! Twitter has been a major contributor to advocacy for our library with all our stakeholders!

Anastasia Hanneken (@21stcentlib), Grade 5–8 school librarian from IMMS Shamong Township, South Dakota

I would not be the librarian I am without the help of social media. Every day, I am inspired by other fantastic educators on Twitter and Facebook. I find out about so many new opportunities such as promotions, contests and educational initiatives. I also use social media to reach my students and parents. I connect with students in a way that was never possible before.

Laura Gardner (@LibrarianMsG), school librarian from Fairhaven, Massachusetts

By using social media, I have been able to connect personally with my PLN to help me learn new techniques, methodologies, and invigorate my classes. As a connected educator, I have been able to connect my students to the outside world through debates, video chats, and even through our classroom social media pages. Students become more engaged and excited about some lessons because they know there is an opportunity to share their work with the outside world. Students are excited about knocking down the walls in our classroom to face real-world learning situations.

AJ Bianco (@AJBianco), Grades 7–8 social studies teacher from New Jersey

By using social media, I have been able to connect personally with my PLN to help me learn new techniques and methodologies and invigorate my classes. As a connected educator, I have been able to connect my students to the outside world through debates, video chats and even through our classroom social media pages. Students become more engaged and excited about some lessons because they know there is an opportunity to share their work with the outside world. Students are excited about knocking down the walls in our classroom to face real-world learning situations.

Julie Boatner (@jboatner), K–5 school librarian from St. Louis, Missouri

We are in the middle of our library program evaluation, and, as a part of that, a survey went out to all the parents in the district. I was surprised to see how many (from K–12) wanted more communication from their children's library. I feel that social media is possibly the best way to do that. Blast out all the awesome things that are happening each day!

Without a doubt, connected librarians equal connected students, connected parents, connected teachers, connected administrators, and connected communities. The learning that occurs from connecting through social media multiplies exponentially as new connections and new learning opportunities reveal themselves through these connections. And it is through these connections that authentic, real-world learning that is relevant and intriguing to students is easily achieved.

CHAPTER 11

Keeping up with Trends

The future of social media and related technologies is changing rapidly. The Pokémon GO app and spin off apps like Harry Potter GO came and went in popularity over one summer before I could even get back to school and start using them in the library. Trying to predict future technology trends is difficult but I see three related trends that are continuing to grow and gain momentum: augmented reality (AR), virtual reality (VR), and mixed reality (MR). The other trend I see on the horizon as more and more schools adopt 1:1 devices and internet access expands across our country is a drastic shift toward individualized learning that will change the landscape of traditional schools as we know them today.

When a librarian friend of mine first mentioned AR and "cool new technology," I was confused. I thought she was referring to Accelerated Reader, K–12 software that had been around for years. Later, I learned about virtual reality and mixed reality and was further confounded. Aren't they all basically the same thing? Let's take a closer look.

Augmented Reality

AR is the integration of digital information and the user's environment in real time. Unlike VR, which creates a totally artificial environment, AR uses the existing environment and overlays new information on top of it by using "trigger" or "target" images that are detected by the AR app and reveal layers of additional information.

The GPS on our smartphones is an example of AR. Have you or your children played a videogame that recognizes your gestures rather than requiring a controller? This is another form of AR. Augmented reality is used to train our military, for medical procedures, construction, car repair, and so much more. School librarians need to be familiar with the changing landscape of AR and assist our students and teachers with using AR.

I am always looking for ways to include AR in the library makerspace and entice teachers into using AR to enhance their curriculum. I've included a few of my favorites here, though this list barely scratches the surface of available AR apps.

> **Aurasma** is one of the first AR apps I used. In its current form, it is glitchy and not the most intuitive AR app I have encountered. I collaborated with Ms. McRae, our biomedical teacher, to bring to life 3-D prints of proteins her students were researching. Using the Aurasma app, Ms. McRae could aim her device at the AR trigger on the printed protein

model, and a student-created video appeared to guide her through that student's research.

Elements 4D lets students explore chemistry through AR. You can print and assemble your own periodic element cubes, or you can purchase wooden cubes from the DAQRI site. (I printed my own using a sturdy card stock.) Students put the cubes together in different configurations to see if there is a reaction when two elements are combined. For instance, when a student puts the oxygen block next to the hydrogen block, water will appear. I guarantee you haven't ever seen kids as excited about the periodic table as they are when using the Elements 4D cubes. DAQRI also provides lesson plans for elementary, middle, and high school students. All of this is absolutely free (except the wooden cubes).

Anatomy 4D has two printable worksheets to use with the Anatomy 4D app: the human body and the heart. The graphics stunning! Students can control which parts of the human body and heart they want to explore. They can turn on (and off) features like the muscular system, veins and arteries, ventricular systems, and so on. The target posters and the app are all free.

ARLOON is another AR app that is specifically geared toward schools. ARLOON contains six different AR experiences designed for primary to secondary students. The six apps cover anatomy, chemistry, geometry, mental math, plants, and the solar system. The cool thing about ARLOON is that students can quiz themselves on their knowledge. The ARLOON app is not free, but it is well worth the minimal cost.

Spacecraft 3D is an AR app developed by the National Aeronautics and Space Administration (NASA); it was introduced to me by a student. The app and target images are both free, and the app allows viewers to see and manipulate various spacecraft designed to study Earth, the moon, Mars, and the universe.

Moonbot Studios brings AR to books, and it is such a treat for kids. According to their website, "Moonbot was founded to tell great stories" and to "change the future of storytelling." Check out their award-winning interactive book *The Fantastic Flying Books of Mr. Morris Lessmore* to see how animation, AR, and interactivity draw readers into the story.

AUGMENTED REALITY RESOURCES

Aurasma (aurasma.com)

Elements 4D (elements4d.daqri.com)

Anatomy 4D (anatomy4d.daqri.com)

ARLOON (arloon.com)

Spacecraft 3D (itunes.apple.com/us/app/spacecraft-3d/id541089908?mt=8)

Moonbot Studios (http://moonbotstudios.com) and *The Fantastic Flying Books of Mr. Morris Lessmore* (moonbotstudios.com/work/the-fantastic-flying-books-of-mr-morris-lessmore)

Virtual Reality

Let's take a look at VR, how it differs from AR, and ways it is (or is expected to be) used in both schools and the workforce.

Virtual reality means experiencing things through our computers that don't really exist. It makes the user feel they are really in a virtual situation, both mentally and physically, and they can move around and explore this interactive computer-created 3-D world.

Perhaps you have been to a theme park where there was a "ride" that let you fly an airplane, go under the sea in a submarine, or ride a roller coaster. Although you never actually left the physical space, the VR experience convinced you otherwise. Full-immersion experiences are necessary for VR to be completely believable, but creating an experience like this would require entire rooms, equipped with hydraulics and other sensors, to meet the VR standards of authentication.

Schools don't have the physical space or the big budgets required for a VR setup like that, but there are more affordable options, like VR headsets, to bring VR into the classroom.

At first glance, VR seems like something more applicable to video game designers than to educators. But consider styles of learning and retention of information—VR allows students to simulate experiences they might not be afforded in real life. Let's take a look at a few ways VR is currently used in schools

Google Expeditions

Imagine choosing from anywhere in the world to take students on a field trip. Google Expeditions are "are collections of linked virtual reality (VR) content and supporting materials that can be used alongside existing curriculum—annotated with details, points of interest, and questions that make them easy to integrate into curriculum already used in schools" (RedboxVR, n.d.)

Virtual Reality in Education

Virtual reality is beginning to make waves in the education space, appealing to educators looking to engage students in a new and innovative way. Several companies are currently leading the market in virtual reality for educational purposes. The following technologies were profiled in a 2016 Touchstore Research blog post.

Immersive VR Education simulates a lecture hall in virtual reality, while adding special effects which can't be utilized in a traditional classroom setting.

Unimersiv is an individualized and immersive VR learning platform offering experiencess such as include exploring the International Space Station, learning about the human body with Anatomy VR, and exploring Stonehenge.

Alchemy VR creates educational virtual reality experiences on an impressive scale, offering a narrative as the user sees and immerses themselves in experiences like exploring the Great Barrier Reef.

zSpace is challenging the assumption that VR technology is antisocial and one-sided, with each user putting on their own headset. zspace users wear glasses similar to 3D glasses that make the content come off the screen for a group of users. zSpace offers content for STEM education, medical training, and more.

Boulevard VR combines art and storytelling in a VR format. Students use this app to explore museums and learn about the installations they see.

EON Reality is looking to change how teachers utilize technology in the classroom. Rather than just consuming premade VR applications, students and teachers can use EON to create their own VR experiences; and it allows for interaction with one another in a VR environment.

Schell Games is one of the largest independent game development companies in the United States. Their VR puzzle game promotes systems thinking and spatial recognition.

ThingLink allows teachers or students to annotate 360°
images with tags or links. Using this technology, students
could look at a 360° picture of Athens, Greece, and click on
different landmarks to see questions, take notes, or follow
links to informative videos and explanations. (Burch, 2016)

VIRTUAL REALITY RESOURCES

Google Expeditions (edu.google.com/expeditions/#about)

Immersive VR Education (immersivevreducation.com)

Unimersiv (unimersiv.com)

Alchemy VR (alchemyvr.com)

zSpace (zspace.com)

Boulevard VR (blvrd.com)

EON Reality (eonreality.com)

Schell Games (schellgames.com)

ThingLink (thinglink.com)

Mixed Reality

Mixed reality (sometimes called hybrid reality or MR) aims to
combine the best aspects of both virtual reality and augmented
reality. In MR environments, users seamlessly navigate through
both the real and virtual environments at the same time.
Instead of residing in an entirely virtual world (i.e. virtual
reality), virtual objects are anchored into a user's real-world
space and augment their real-world environment, making
virtual interactions appear to be "real." These interactions

mimic our natural behavior of interaction, such as objects getting bigger as you get closer and the changing of perspectives as you move around an object.

MR is currently being touted as the most important emerging technology—the next big paradigm shift—in education. One way MR could accomplish this shift is through the way students and teachers will be able to use MR to communicate. Something known as holoportation (a type of 3D capture technology) could allow students from all around the world to interact and learn in the same virtual space. Here are a few examples of emerging MR geared toward education:

Project Esper was designed to provide detailed anatomical models for medical students. It has far-reaching applications for medical professionals: it could eliminate the need for cadavers in medical school labs, and doctors could use it to explain ailments to patients.

Curiscope pairs an AR/VR app with a special shirt (a Virtuali-Tee), allowing students the opportunity to learn about the human body in a fun and creative way.

ZapBox is an MR headset that allows you to do things like create a painting in a 3D space and walk around it, or send a probe to Mars.

Bridge is an MR/VR headset designed specifically for the iPhone. It includes a depth sensor that stabilizes AR objects so they appear to be a part of the real world around you. This is a fancy way of saying that Bridge offers users an incredibly realistic MR experience.

You may be wondering if there is a relationship between AR, VR, MR, and social media. The answer is: a big one. When Mark Zuckerberg, founder of Facebook, is already using devices like Oculus to create VR social rooms, you have to take note.

MIXED REALITY RESOURCES

Project Esper (3d4medical.com/lab)

Curisope (curiscope.com)

ZapBox (zappar.com/zapbox)

Bridge (bridge.occipital.com)

A quote I have always loved and think is appropriate here comes from Thomas C. Murray (@thomascmurray), Director of Innovation for Future Ready Schools at the Alliance for Excellent Education in Washington, DC. Murray observes that, "the technology your kids are using today will be the worst technology they ever use."

Like it or not, technology is changing the way our children learn and interact. In a not so distant future, schools will change from the institutions we've known them to be, shedding the confinement of buildings, rooms, and desks, and enveloping a global, socialized learning experience from our own homes. Independent, individualized learning will follow, free from the current confines of age-based grade levels. Students will be free to learn and pursue their own genius with teachers and class-mates from across the globe. Once this is achieved, I predict the world will experience a revolution in technology and science that will take us, our global community, to heights we can't even possibly imagine.

As we have whenever new technologies come through the doors of our schools, school librarians will lead the way. Administrators, teachers, students, and parents will be counting on us to demon-strate and model the effective use of these technologies in support of the curriculum, whatever that may look like in the future.

Conclusion

While writing this book I would frequently pose questions about various aspects of social media in schools to my PLN. Sadly, the overwhelming response from school librarians and other educators from across the United States and around the world was one of blocking and overly restrictive internet access.

For those who are nodding their heads, frustrated that they too are in this all too familiar situation I say this to you: as school librarians, we are the voice, the advocate for our students and teachers. Speak up for what you know is best for students (and teachers). Learning in the isolation of the walls of our schools is not learning. Learning takes place when you can connect, engage, swap ideas, share, and collaborate with others who bring a different world view. Access to and use of social media tools is the way we can connect and empower our students to broaden their learning experiences and to become masters of their own learning. We are the squeaky wheel that will not and must not be silenced, for the sake of our students and the sake of our future.

References

Adams, H. (2010). www.aasl.ala.org/aaslblog/?p=1262

Alter, A. (2012). The Weird World of Fan Fiction. Retrieved from www.wsj.com/articles/SB10001424052702303734204577464411825970488

Angove, A. (2013). What Is Flipboard? Retrieved from www.whistleout.com/CellPhones/Guides/What-is-Flipboard

Barseghian, T. (2011). Straight from the DOE: Dispelling myths about blocked sites. Retrieved from ww2.kqed.org/mindshift/2011/04/26/straight-from-the-doe-facts-about-blocking-sites-in-schools

Burch, A, (2016). The Top 10 Companies Working on Education in Virtual Reality and Augmented Reality. Retrieved from touchstoneresearch.com/the-top-10-companies-working-on-education-in-virtual-reality-and-augmented-reality/

Craig, R. (2015). The New Digital Stars of Higher Education. Retrieved from techcrunch.com/2015/12/07/the-new-digital-stars-of-higher-education

Crescerence. (2015). 3 Ways Snapchat Can Help Schools Engage With Students. Retrieved from crescerance.com/3-ways-snapchat-can-help-schools-engage-with-students.

Delzer, K. (2016). Three Reasons Students Should Own Your Classroom's Twitter and Instagram Accounts (EdSurge News). Retrieved from www.edsurge.com/news/2016-02-03-three-reasons-students-should-own-your-classroom-s-twitter-and-instagram-accounts

Educational Technology & Mobile Learning. 2017. The Complete Guide to Skype in Education. Retrieved from www.educatorstechnology.com/2012/06/complete-guide-to-use-of-skype-in.html

Educause. (2012). 7 Things you should know about flipped classrooms. Retrieved from library.educause.edu/~/media/files/library/2012/2/eli7081-pdf.pdf

Gangwar, A. (2017). 5 Best Yik Yak Alternatives You Should Check Out. Retrieved from beebom.com/best-yik-yak-alternatives

Gibson, S. (2015). How could Periscope be used in Education? Retrieved from educatingtomorrowslearners.blogspot.com/2015/04/how-could-periscope-be-used-in-education.html

Greenwood, S.; Perrin, A; Duggan, M. (2016). Social Media Update 2016. Retrieved fromwww.pewinternet.org/2016/11/11/social-media-update-2016

Gutenberg, P. (n.d.). Fan fiction. Retrieved May 11, 2017, from self.gutenberg.org/articles/eng/Fan_fiction

Hamilton, B. (2017). Passages of Promise: A Student eBook Anthology of Creative Writing. Retrieved from theunquietlibrarian.wordpress.com/tag/ebook

Hiskey, J. (2010). Why Soap Operas Are Called Soap Operas. Retrived from www.todayifoundout.com/index.php/2010/06/why-soap-operas-are-called-soap-operas

(iFolio. (2016). Digital Portfolio College Admission Summer Programs | iFolio. Retrieved from www.ifoliocorp.com/summerprograms-2017/

Jaschik, S. (2015). Admissions Revolution. Retrieved from www.insidehighered.com/news/2015/09/29/80-colleges-

and-universities-announce-plan-new-application-and-new-approach

Jones, G. (2017). 12 Easy Instagram Library & Literacy Promotion Ideas. Retrieved from yalsa.ala.org/blog/2017/02/23/12-insta-easy-instagram-library-literacy-promotion-ideas

Kowalczyk, P. (2017). 15 most popular fiction websites. Retrieved from ebookfriendly.com/fan-fiction-websites

Lofton, J. (2016). The #SWVBC: Connecting Library Clubs Across The Country. Retrieved from www.mackintysl.com/the-swvbc-connecting-library-clubs-across-the-country

Microsoft. (2017). Mystery Skype. Retrieved from education.microsoft.com/skype-in-the-classroom/mystery-skype

Miller, M. (2017). 15 ways to use Snapchat in classes and schools. Retrieved from ditchthattextbook.com/2016/04/11/15-ways-to-use-snapchat-in-classes-and-schools

Modo Labs, Inc. (2016). Social Media Use Among College Students and Teens – What's In, What's Out and Why. Retrieved from www.modolabs.com/blog-post/social-media-use-among-college-students-and-teens-whats-in-whats-out-and-why

Moreau, E. (2017). 10 Social Apps That Let You Share and Interact Anonymously. Retrieved from www.lifewire.com/top-anonymous-social-networking-apps-3485942

MTV. (2017). Sexting in America: When Privates Go Public. [News Video] Retrieved from www.mtv.com/videos/news/483801/sexting-in-america-when-privates-go-public-part-1.jhtml

Nokleby, M. (2012) Share It! Publishing Student Work Online: Michele Nokleby ... [YouTube Video] Retrieved from www.youtube.com/watch?v=A-eRv7DRoiA.

RedboxVR. (n.d.). What Is Expeditions? Retrieved from redboxvr.co.uk/overview.html

Sidney, R. (2016). Best-Selling Children's Book Author Spills the Tea on Self-Publishing. Retrieved from nelsonbeatstheodds. wordpress.com/2016/10/22/best-selling-childrens-book-author

Soka Gakkai International. (2005). Daisaku Ikeda: Buddhist philosopher, peacebuilder, and educator. Retrieved from www.daisakuikeda.org

StoryWars.net. (n.d.) Abot Story Wars. Retrieved from https:// www.storywars.net/about

U.S. Department of Education. (2017). Reimagining the Role of Technology in Education: 2017 National Education Technology Plan Update. Office of Educational Technology : Washington, D.C.

Wetta, M. (2016). All about Instagram. School Library Journal blog. Retrieved from www.slj.com/2016/02/technology/ all-about-instagram/#_

APPENDIX A
ISTE Standards

ISTE Standards for Students

The ISTE Standards for Students emphasize the skills and qualities we want for students, enabling them to engage and thrive in a connected, digital world. The standards are designed for use by educators across the curriculum, with every age student, with a goal of cultivating these skills throughout a student's academic career.

1. **Empowered Learner**
   Students leverage technology to take an active role in choosing, achieving and demonstrating competency in their learning goals, informed by the learning sciences. Students:

   a. articulate and set personal learning goals, develop strategies leveraging technology to achieve them and reflect on the learning process itself to improve learning outcomes.

   b. build networks and customize their learning environments in ways that support the learning process.

   c. use technology to seek feedback that informs and improves their practice and to demonstrate their learning in a variety of ways.

   d. understand the fundamental concepts of technology operations, demonstrate the ability to choose, use and troubleshoot current technologies and are able to transfer their knowledge to explore emerging technologies.

2. **Digital Citizen**
   Students recognize the rights, responsibilities and opportunities of living, learning and working in an interconnected

digital world, and they act and model in ways that are safe, legal and ethical. Students:

a. cultivate and manage their digital identity and reputation and are aware of the permanence of their actions in the digital world.

b. engage in positive, safe, legal and ethical behavior when using technology, including social interactions online or when using networked devices.

c. demonstrate an understanding of and respect for the rights and obligations of using and sharing intellectual property.

d. manage their personal data to maintain digital privacy and security and are aware of data-collection technology used to track their navigation online.

3. Knowledge Constructor

Students critically curate a variety of resources using digital tools to construct knowledge, produce creative artifacts and make meaningful learning experiences for themselves and others. Students:

a. plan and employ effective research strategies to locate information and other resources for their intellectual or creative pursuits.

b. evaluate the accuracy, perspective, credibility and relevance of information, media, data or other resources.

c. curate information from digital resources using a variety of tools and methods to create collections of artifacts that demonstrate meaningful connections or conclusions.

d. build knowledge by actively exploring real-world issues and problems, developing ideas and theories and pursuing answers and solutions.

4. Innovative Designer

Students use a variety of technologies within a design process to identify and solve problems by creating new, useful or imaginative solutions. Students:

a. know and use a deliberate design process for generating ideas, testing theories, creating innovative artifacts or solving authentic problems.

b. select and use digital tools to plan and manage a design process that considers design constraints and calculated risks.

c. develop, test and refine prototypes as part of a cyclical design process.

d. exhibit a tolerance for ambiguity, perseverance and the capacity to work with open-ended problems.

5. Computational Thinker

Students develop and employ strategies for understanding and solving problems in ways that leverage the power of technological methods to develop and test solutions. Students:

a. formulate problem definitions suited for technology-assisted methods such as data analysis, abstract models and algorithmic thinking in exploring and finding solutions.

b. collect data or identify relevant data sets, use digital tools to analyze them, and represent data in various ways to facilitate problem-solving and decision-making.

c. break problems into component parts, extract key information, and develop descriptive models to understand complex systems or facilitate problem-solving.

d. understand how automation works and use algorithmic thinking to develop a sequence of steps to create and test automated solutions.

6. Creative Communicator

Students communicate clearly and express themselves creatively for a variety of purposes using the platforms, tools, styles, formats and digital media appropriate to their goals. Students:

a. choose the appropriate platforms and tools for meeting the desired objectives of their creation or communication.

b. create original works or responsibly repurpose or remix digital resources into new creations.

c. communicate complex ideas clearly and effectively by creating or using a variety of digital objects such as visualizations, models or simulations.

d. publish or present content that customizes the message and medium for their intended audiences.

7. Global Collaborator

Students use digital tools to broaden their perspectives and enrich their learning by collaborating with others and working effectively in teams locally and globally. Students:

a. use digital tools to connect with learners from a variety of backgrounds and cultures, engaging with them in ways that broaden mutual understanding and learning.

b. use collaborative technologies to work with others, including peers, experts or community members, to examine issues and problems from multiple viewpoints.

c. contribute constructively to project teams, assuming various roles and responsibilities to work effectively toward a common goal.

d. explore local and global issues and use collaborative technologies to work with others to investigate solutions.

© 2016 International Society for Technology in Education.

ISTE Standards for Educators

The ISTE Standards for Educators are your road map to helping students become empowered learners. These standards will deepen your practice, promote collaboration with peers, challenge you to rethink traditional approaches and prepare students to drive their own learning.

Empowered Professional

1. Learner

Educators continually improve their practice by learning from and with others and exploring proven and promising practices that leverage technology to improve student learning. Educators:

a. Set professional learning goals to explore and apply pedagogical approaches made possible by technology and reflect on their effectiveness.

b. Pursue professional interests by creating and actively participating in local and global learning networks.

c. Stay current with research that supports improved student learning outcomes, including findings from the learning sciences.

2. Leader

Educators seek out opportunities for leadership to support student empowerment and success and to improve teaching and learning. Educators:

a. Shape, advance and accelerate a shared vision for empowered learning with technology by engaging with education stakeholders.

b. Advocate for equitable access to educational technology, digital content and learning opportunities to meet the diverse needs of all students.

    c. Model for colleagues the identification, exploration, evaluation, curation and adoption of new digital resources and tools for learning.

3. Citizen

Educators inspire students to positively contribute to and responsibly participate in the digital world. Educators:

    a. Create experiences for learners to make positive, socially responsible contributions and exhibit empathetic behavior online that build relationships and community.

    b. Establish a learning culture that promotes curiosity and critical examination of online resources and fosters digital literacy and media fluency.

    c. Mentor students in safe, legal and ethical practices with digital tools and the protection of intellectual rights and property.

    d. Model and promote management of personal data and digital identity and protect student data privacy.

Learning Catalyst

4. Collaborator

Educators dedicate time to collaborate with both colleagues and students to improve practice, discover and share resources and ideas, and solve problems. Educators:

    a. Dedicate planning time to collaborate with colleagues to create authentic learning experiences that leverage technology.

    b. Collaborate and co-learn with students to discover and use new digital resources and diagnose and troubleshoot technology issues.

    c. Use collaborative tools to expand students' authentic, real-world learning experiences by engaging virtually with experts, teams and students, locally and globally.

    d. Demonstrate cultural competency when communicating with students, parents and colleagues and interact with them as co-collaborators in student learning.

5. Designer

Educators design authentic, learner-driven activities and environments that recognize and accommodate learner variability. Educators:

    a. Use technology to create, adapt and personalize learning experiences that foster independent learning and accommodate learner differences and needs.

    b. Design authentic learning activities that align with content area standards and use digital tools and resources to maximize active, deep learning.

    c. Explore and apply instructional design principles to create innovative digital learning environments that engage and support learning.

6. Facilitator

Educators facilitate learning with technology to support student achievement of the 2016 ISTE Standards for Students. Educators:

    a. Foster a culture where students take ownership of their learning goals and outcomes in both independent and group settings.

    b. Manage the use of technology and student learning strategies in digital platforms, virtual environments, hands-on makerspaces or in the field.

    c. Create learning opportunities that challenge students to use a design process and computational thinking to innovate and solve problems.

    d. Model and nurture creativity and creative expression to communicate ideas, knowledge or connections.

7. Analyst

Educators understand and use data to drive their instruction and support students in achieving their learning goals. Educators:

a. Provide alternative ways for students to demonstrate competency and reflect on their learning using technology.

b. Use technology to design and implement a variety of formative and summative assessments that accommodate learner needs, provide timely feedback to students and inform instruction.

c. Use assessment data to guide progress and communicate with students, parents and education stakeholders to build student self-direction.

© 2017 International Society for Technology in Education.